WORK EXPERIENCE

ACTIVITY PACK

supporting the *SEN Press* 'Work Experience' series ...

WWW.SENPRESS.CO.UK

Introduction

ABOUT SEN PRESS

Since its launch in June 2006, *SEN Press* has quickly established itself in the field of special needs education. Concentrating initially on the 'transition' years (14-19), and the twin fields of Life Skills and Literacy, it now has over two dozen age-appropriate readers available that support ASDAN and other established Life Skills and Social Skills courses.

SEN Press is currently developing a set of Activity Packs (interactive CDs with Teacher Notes) to accompany each series of books, starting with Work Experience.

All resources may be viewed and ordered through the website: **www.senpress.co.uk**

The publisher's founder and owner, Peter Clarke, has taught for twenty years in the fields of literacy and special education. He has also had first-hand experience of bringing up his Down's Syndrome son, Adam, who, thanks to an excellent education, is now able to hold down a simple, unpaid job and travel independently on the bus.

SEN Press publications are endorsed by ASDAN

www.asdan.co.uk

browse and order at
www.senpress.co.uk

Phone 01422 844822
Email peterclarke@senpress.co.uk
Address 7 Cliffe Street, Hebden Bridge, West Yorkshire HX7 8BY

Work Experience Activity Pack
Published: January 2008. Reprinted April 2008.
ISBN: 978-1-905579-55-6 © SEN Press 2008
A CIP record of this publication is available from the British Library.
(Schools are free to photocopy materials in this publication for use in class or for homework.)

SITE LICENCE INCLUDED.

Minimum PC system requirements to run the interactive CD-ROM are:
Pentium II 600 Mhz
128 Mb RAM
16x CD-ROM drive
16 bit colour display

Minimum Mac system requirements to run the interactive CD-ROM are:
G3 Processor or higher
Mac OSX 10.1.5 or higher
256MB RAM
16-bit Color
16-bit sound card
16x CD-ROM

ACKNOWLEDGEMENTS

I have received a lot of help in developing the Work Experience books and the Activity Pack, so my thanks go to :

Ian Hunt, Duncan Witham, Shaun Rafferty and Joe Butcher at *Q&D Multimedia* in Derby

Catherine Burch, my editor and project manager at *Cambridge Publishing Management*

Janie Nicholas, marketing consultant

Special Needs teachers: Kelso Peel and Christine Richardson (Rochdale), Jayne Cowdale (Wolverhampton) and Sophia England (London)

Heather Fry at *ASDAN* in Bristol

Authors and illustrators of this series: Kathryn Baker (*Sylvie Poggio Illustration Agency*), Bob Moulder, Jean de Lemos, Sarah Wimperis, Sue Woollatt, (*Graham-Cameron Illustration Agency*) and Sue Graves (author)

Ruth Cooper, *Connexions* officer in Rochdale, Lancashire.

Peter Clarke, Publisher

CONTENTS

1. INTRODUCTION

About *SEN Press* i
Contents ii
Preface iii
About these Resources:
  - The CD-ROM iv
  - The Teacher Book iv
  - The 'Work Experience' reading books and where to buy them iv
  - The Interactive Activities v
  - The Resource Sheets vi
Key buttons and icons in the Interactive Activities .... vii-ix
Lesson Planning: suggestions for using the Activity Pack x
Reading Ages x

2. A SUPERMARKET

The book 1
Page-by-page notes 2-4
Interactive Activities 5-10
Resource Sheets 11-19

3. A FAST-FOOD RESTAURANT

The book 20
Page-by-page notes 21-23
Interactive Activities 24-27
Resource Sheets 28-37

4. A CHARITY SHOP

The book 38
Page-by-page notes 39-41
Interactive Activities 42-45
Resource Sheets 46-55

5. A GARAGE

The book 56
Page-by-page notes 57-59
Interactive Activities 60-63
Resource Sheets 64-73

6. AN ANIMAL CHARITY

The book 74
Page-by-page notes 75-77
Interactive Activities 78-81
Resource Sheets 82-91

7. AN INTERVIEW

The book 92
Page-by-page notes 93-95
Interactive Activities 96-99
Resource Sheets 100-112

PREFACE

Preparing students for work experience

For most SEN students, work experience will be one of the biggest challenges they will have faced. It comes as they approach school leaving, and it will be their ability to adapt to the new demands of work that could mean the difference between a sheltered life of dependency and one of greater community involvement, independence and self-fulfilment.

Many SEN students *will* be able to hold down a simple job, perhaps unpaid, perhaps part-time, if

- The right skills are developed in each student
- They know what to expect, and what is expected of them
- Employers are patient and are prepared to take longer to train them
- There is belief in them.

The books in the SEN Press *Work Experience* series attempt to paint an honest picture of work experience and the many different factors that affect the students. They cover

- Some of the many anxieties inevitably felt by the students. For example: being in totally unfamiliar surroundings; not knowing anyone to talk to at breaks or lunchtimes; not knowing what to do or how to do it; fear of failure; being told off
- Tiredness after a day at work
- The many positives, too: students overcoming these anxieties; coping; feeling proud of their achievements; developing greater independence, self-confidence and social skills.

This Activity Pack provides students with opportunities for reinforcing literacy and numeracy skills; for discussion and further instruction; many relevant Interactive Activities, a number of Resource Sheets, and role play and research suggestions for follow-up work. It also provides the teacher with a highly flexible resource suitable for group and individual work.

Introduction

ABOUT THESE RESOURCES

This *Work Experience Activity Pack* complements the six SEN Press 'Work Experience' titles available in January 2008...

- *A Supermarket*
- *A Fast-Food Restaurant*
- *A Charity Shop*
- *A Garage*
- *An Animal Charity*
- *An Interview*

...and provides the teacher with a course for students at Entry Level 1-2.

It affords the teacher two big advantages:

- The facility to give whiteboard lessons
- The facility to make and save changes to the text, so teachers can make abridged or personalised versions for individual students

The Pack contains a CD-ROM and a Teacher's Book of notes and Resource Sheets.

THE CD-ROM

The CD-ROM contains the text and illustrations for all six *Work Experience* titles and a wealth of other classroom resources:

- **Spoken text versions** of the books, with **editable text** so teachers can write personalised versions of the stories for individual pupils
- 19 **Interactive Activities** (listed in full below)
- **Teaching objectives**
- **Resource Sheets** in pdf format (comprehension, flashcards, wordsearch, spot the difference, sheets for evaluation and record-keeping).

THE TEACHER BOOK

This contains introductions to the course as a whole and notes on the individual titles:

- Page-by-page teacher notes for the books
- Explanations of the CD-ROM's basic functions
- Notes on the Interactive Activities (see below)
- Hard copies of the Resource Sheets (see below)
- Ideas for discussion and further activities

Hard copies of all the Resource Sheets are included for schools to photocopy freely.

THE READERS

The activities in this Pack are designed to work with and alongside these six reading books. They are available singly or in money-saving packs of 6.

Contact our distributor:
Phone: 01904 431213
Fax: 01904 430868
Email: orders@yps-publishing.co.uk

Or visit our website:
www.senpress.co.uk

Single copy:
978-1-905579-29-7
Value Pack (6 copies):
978-1-905579-31-0

Single copy:
978-1-905579-03-7
Value Pack (6 copies):
978-1-905579-13-6

Single copy:
978-1-905579-07-5
Value Pack (6 copies):
978-1-905579-17-4

Single copy:
978-1-905579-21-1
Value Pack (6 copies):
978-1-905579-23-5

Single copy:
978-1-905579-22-8
Value Pack (6 copies):
978-1-905579-24-2

Single copy:
978-1-905579-30-3
Value Pack (6 copies):
978-1-905579-32-7

Browse and buy at
www.senpress.co.uk

Read more about our other series:
Everyday Challenges, Scary Things, Simple Meals, Ups and Downs.

Introduction

THE INTERACTIVE ACTIVITIES

The topics of the 19 Interactive Activities included on the CD are set out in the box below. They have been spread across all six titles, and fall into three main categories:

K = key activities that will apply to ALL placements

M = activities that will apply to MANY different placements

S = activities that are SPECIFIC to a particular type of job or placement

BOOK TITLE	INTERACTIVE ACTIVITIES	
A Supermarket:	Golden Rules	K
	Bag packing	S
	Sell-by dates	S
	Signs and aisles	S
A Fast-Food Restaurant	What to wear	K
	The working day	K
	Hygiene	M
A Charity Shop	Health & safety	K
	Dealing with customers	M
	Labels and sorting	S
A Garage	The employer's point of view	K
	What to expect	K
	Learning by watching	K
An Animal Charity	Arranging your own placement	K
	Working outdoors	M
	Working with animals	S
An Interview	Getting there on time	K
	Giving a good impression	K
	What happens at an interview	K

These activities will introduce students to the essentials and make them think; they will also provide valuable skill-reinforcement in other areas of the curriculum, such as maths, literacy, drama, PSHE and citizenship.

Introduction

THE RESOURCE SHEETS FOR THE STUDENT

You are free to copy these sheets freely for use in your school.

There are seven resource sheets for each book and two additional resource sheets for the course as a whole.

FOR EACH BOOK...

1. How well did you read?
10 simple true or false questions related to the text.

2. Flashcards
Sixteen work-related words taken from the text (to be printed out and cut up by the teacher).

3. Wordsearch
10 key words chosen from the 16 flashcards.

4. 'Spot the Difference'
An illustration from the book with 6 details changed.

5. The book and the activities feedback sheet
Students are given the opportunity to write a sentence or two giving their views on both the book they've just read and the activities they have undertaken.

6. How well did the character in the book do?
Students fill in an evaluation form for the student they've just read about.

7. Student's record sheet
A record sheet for the teacher to complete which records the activities undertaken by the student for each part of the course, and the level achieved.

FOR THE COURSE AS A WHOLE....

1. Details of my placement
A sheet for the student to record, beforehand, all the details of his/her placement eg breaks and lunchtimes, getting there, what to take etc.

2. My work experience: how I got on
The student records how he/she got on, lessons learned, likes and dislikes etc.

Introduction

KEY TO BUTTONS AND ICONS IN THE INTERACTIVE ACTIVITIES

GENERAL

 Click on a book cover to read that story.

  Takes you to a menu of all the activities on the CD-ROM. They are colour coded related to the number of placements they would be relevant to: red for all placements, blue for many placements and yellow for specific placements.

  Takes you to a menu of PDF worksheets and other resources.

  Takes you to the settings screen where you can turn audio on or off for the whole CD-ROM or activate a darker panel around the text to make it easier to read.

  Information about this product. (NOTE: In some activities this button will bring up a word definition)

  Information about the publisher.

  Will exit the program.

  This will take you out of an activity back to the story if that is how you got to the activity.

  This will take you out of an activity back to the activities menu if that is how you got to the activity.

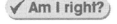 Will play the audio again. (This button is only available when the audio is activated.)

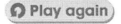 Move on to the next screen.

  Click this to find out if your have completed an exercise correctly.

  Click this to repeat an exercise. The content will often change to provide some variety.

Will provide simple assistance if you get stuck or forget what to do.

Introduction

 Closes a pop-up box or panel.

 Tells you how far through the activity you are. Each spot represents a screen.

STORY CONTROLS

 Returns to the cover of the book.

 Turns on a page.

 Turns back a page.

 Allows you to alter the text in the story.

 Deletes all text on the page so you can add your own.

 Reverts to the original text.

SPECIAL TEACHER CONTROLS

 Mutes the audio.

 Turns muted audio back on.

 (Stories only) Saves edited text. This allows you to create personalised versions. A system dialog box will open to allow you to save to your computer.

Introduction

 (Stories only) Loads previously saved edited text. Find the version you want via the system dialog box that opens.

 Brings up a reminder of an associated page from a story.

 Skips forward a screen.

 Skips back a screen.

Teacher notes Brings up teacher notes for an activity.

Prompts (Stories only) Reveals discussion points related to each page.

NOTE If any button appears black and has no icon, that function is not currently available.

Introduction

LESSON PLANNING

SUGGESTIONS FOR USING THE WORK EXPERIENCE ACTIVITY PACK

It would be impractical to suggest a single plan for teachers to follow.

Here are some alternatives to consider.

- The course could be covered intensively in 6 weeks or half a term, covering one title every week.
- Alternatively, it could be spread over a 12-week term, allowing two weeks to cover each title.
- Teachers may choose a single title, *A Supermarket* for example, to introduce the subject of work experience at the beginning of the year, and introduce other titles at a more leisurely pace throughout the year.

However spaced out the coverage might be, teachers might consider these ideas for individual lessons.

1. **Start with a whiteboard lesson (approx. 20 mins) for the first run through of each title.**

   Use the audio track of the book, pausing and asking questions, examining the illustrations, focusing on one or two key issues.

2. **Follow-up, the next day, with a second group read-through.**

   Use the books themselves, or use the CD-ROM's 'write-your-own-simplified text' facility with individual students.

3. **For the rest of the week/fortnight/month set aside time for follow-up reading and vocabulary work.**

   Also discussion, the Interactive Activities, the various resource sheets, spreading over into other lessons for topics, such as *time* and *money* (Maths) or role-play situations (Drama). There will also be opportunities for students to do their own research.

4. **Give students Work Experience folders to collect the work they have covered with the resource sheets.**

   For example, the details they assemble for their own placements, the various evaluation sheets, the social sight vocabulary on the flashcards, the student record sheet that will keep a record of the student's achievements.

READING AGES

Title	Fry Readability Graph	Flesch-Kincaid formula	Average reading age
A Supermarket	6.8	6.1	6.5
A Fast-Food Restaurant	7.1	6.5	6.8
A Charity Shop	7.9	7.7	7.8
A Garage	6.8	6.4	6.6
An Animal Charity	7.5	7.8	7.7
An Interview	6.5	5.9	6.2

These are the reading age figures calculated for the individual 'Work Experience' titles using two well established formulae.

The less precise figure of 7.0 - 8.0 years is given elsewhere in these notes. Of course other factors such as the amount of text on a page, its layout, the choice of font and the number of illustrations affect readability, some improving it and others adversely affecting it. On balance my feeling is that the calculated reading ages of 6.2 and 6.5 are artificially low for texts of 500 words or more, and I have therefore made adjustments based on my own knowledge and experience. I would be glad to hear teachers' views on this when they have used the materials in the classroom.

RESOURCES FOR 'A SUPERMARKET'

'A SUPERMARKET'

WORK EXPERIENCE SERIES

LEVEL: 1-2

READING AGE: 7.0 – 8.0 YEARS

24 PAGES

600 WORDS

KEY THEMES

Working in a busy environment.

Learning the layout of a big store.

Staff facilities.

'Golden rules'.

Sorting skills.

Dealing with customers.

THE NARRATIVE

Philip is doing work experience at his local supermarket.

It's a huge, busy store in which to work but he has an induction from Donna, his supervisor, and he has Elaine to help him for te first week. After that he's on his own. Apart from the day when his mates drop by and distract him, he tries hard and is polite and helpful to customers. He has difficulty, however, with arranging food items by their sell-by dates, and remembering the entry code for getting into the staffroom.

More issues are touched on in the narrative, and teachers are given 'prompts' at the top corner of each right-hand page to remind them of points they could develop as they read through the book.

Resources for: 'A Supermarket'

PAGE BY PAGE NOTES FOR THE TEACHER

A SUPERMARKET: PAGE 1

- Identify the key features in the illustration.
- Comment on the name of the supermarket (many of the boys will have heard of "the Premier League" in football).
- Talk about Philip's appearance (uniform, tie, badge etc) and his feelings about working there.
- How would the students feel working there?
- List the supermarkets in the neighbourhood and others the students may have heard of, and consider similarities and differences and views about each.

A SUPERMARKET: PAGES 2-3

- Think about Philip's morning routine and how he can be ready for Elaine.
- Question students about their morning routine.
- Examine 'Getting There on Time' Interactive Activity - see page 97.
- What Philip will need to get ready to take with him.
- 'Leg-pulling' and how to tell if someone is being serious or not.

A SUPERMARKET: PAGES 4-5

- Explain what is meant by 'induction'.
- Who wears identity badges and what are they for?
- Talk about uniforms and why they're worn. (See 'What to Wear' Interactive Activity - see page 25.)
- The challenge for the student of trying to remember everything he/she is told.
- The difficulties of working in a very busy environment.

A SUPERMARKET: PAGES 6-7

- Talk about how goods are arranged in supermarkets.
- Look at the 'Signs & Aisles' Interactive Activity - page 10.

2

Resources for: 'A Supermarket'

A SUPERMARKET: PAGES 8-9

- Talk about PIN numbers. What are they?
- Recognise other features in the illustration (eg fire hose, 'Staff Only' sign).

A SUPERMARKET: PAGES 10-11

- Look at the 'Golden Rules' Interactive Activity - page 6.
- What is a work staffroom for?
- What will happen at breaks and lunchtimes?
- What do the notices on the board say?

A SUPERMARKET: PAGES 12-13

- Discuss shelf stacking and what it involves.
- What are perishable goods?
- Look at the 'Sell-by Dates' Interactive Activity - see page 9 for teacher notes.

A SUPERMARKET: PAGES 14-15

- Talk about students having to cope on their own.
- Customers and how to deal with rudeness.
- What 'the customer is always right' means.
- See 'Dealing with Customers' Interactive Activity - page 44.
- The importance of not taking rudeness personally.
- Discuss the possible consequences of 'answering back'.

A SUPERMARKET: PAGES 16-17

- What should you report to your supervisor?
- When should you ask for help?

Resources for: 'A Supermarket'

A SUPERMARKET: PAGES 18-19

- Look at the 'Bag Packing' Interactive Activity - see page 8.
- Go through the main principles of packing shopping bags.
- Discuss how people can be 'too helpful' – see also the 'Golden Rules' Interactive Activity - see page 6.

A SUPERMARKET: PAGES 20-21

- Stress the importance of dissuading friends from dropping by during working hours.
- Talk about rules at work (including the use of mobile phones).

A SUPERMARKET: PAGES 22-23

- Discuss what is happening in the illustrations (there is no explanation in text).
- Safe and sensible ways of lifting.
- Asking others to help.
- The temptation to be 'macho' and want to prove yourself.

A SUPERMARKET: PAGE 24

- Discuss how well Philip did.
- Evaluate Philip's performance using the "How well did Philip do?" Resource Sheet on page 17.

INTERACTIVE ACTIVITIES

There are four interactive activities that develop key themes in the narrative. They are designed for use both on whiteboards and individual PCs.

1. GOLDEN RULES

This activity picks up on an important feature in the book – rules (at work). Students will discover that the three rules ("be punctual, be polite, be helpful" – the supermarket's motto) may need a bit more thinking about than they thought when asked to consider different everyday situations.

See page 6 for full details of this Interactive Activity.

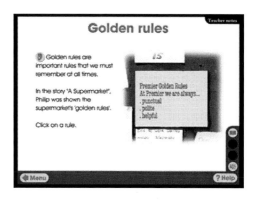

2. BAG-PACKING

In the book, Philip helped customers to pack their bags at the checkout. This exercise is designed to get students to consider sensible ways of separating different categories of goods (hard/heavy, soft/breakable, smelly) when packing at a check-out.

See page 8 for full details of this Interactive Activity.

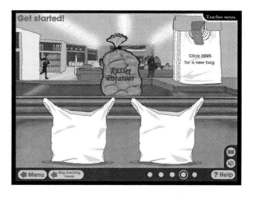

3. SELL-BY DATES

In the book, Philip struggles to understand sell-by dates on food packaging. In this activity, students are challenged to arrange such goods on the shelves, so the oldest are at the front and the newest at the back.

See page 9 for full details of this Interactive Activity.

4. SIGNS AND AISLES

This activity will get students to take notice of and learn to read supermarket signs that will help them to understand how goods are arranged/grouped and to locate particular items with greater confidence.

See page 10 for full details of this Interactive Activity.

Resources for: 'A Supermarket'

1. 'GOLDEN RULES' INTERACTIVE ACTIVITY TEACHER NOTES

> **RELATES TO: 'A SUPERMARKET' PAGES 10-11**
>
> **LEVEL: 1-2**
>
> ### OBJECTIVES
>
> - To introduce a useful framework ('Golden Rules') for a discussion on the key qualities expected of students at work.
> - To test the student's understanding of what the terms 'punctual', 'polite' and 'helpful' mean in everyday situations.
>
> ### FOLLOW-UP ACTIVITIES
>
> - Think up 'Golden Rules' for the school or class.
> - Work out with the student appropriate 'Golden Rules' for his/her work placement (maybe requiring one or two changes to these 'golden rules').
> - Role play (using the different situations included).

PART 1: BE PUNCTUAL
SUGGESTIONS FOR DISCUSSION/FOLLOW-UP ACTIVITIES

- Discuss *why* punctuality is a 'Golden Rule' at work.
- Discuss what to do if you're going to be late on your work experience.
- Use the times of day mentioned in the text (eg. Philip's start time, his morning and afternoon break times) as an opportunity for reinforcing telling the time.
- Recall, if applicable, a school trip or another group activity when someone was late and everyone else was held up, or someone had forgotten something and departure had to be delayed.
- Consider various role play situations about punctuality: eg a school trip delayed because one of the students is late; a situation on a work placement where a student is persistently late; arriving late for a film.
- Suggest a short piece of writing about being late for something important.
- Discuss the *reasons* for arriving 10 minutes early for work. For instance time taken to smarten yourself up; to go to the toilet; to put your coat/bag away in a locker; to 'clock in'; to meet with your supervisor; to be generally ready.
- Discuss journey preparation for work experience. Go over, with the student, the time that each part of the journey to work may take, and making an allowance for possible delays.
- Written work - the student writes down his/her travel schedule to get to work on time (with help).
- You can also use the 'Getting There on Time' activity in *An Interview* here. See page 96.
- Discuss the exception to the rule (parties), and the reasons for it.
- Discuss with students any parties they've been to recently or parties they can remember.
- Discuss any cinema trips undertaken by the students. Ask them why they should arrive a few minutes early. For instance extra time for queues at the ticket office, especially for popular, recently issued films. Also time to buy sweets, popcorn, drink or to go to the toilet before the film starts.
- Mention trailers and adverts that precede the main film, allowing people to arrive a few minutes later than the published start-time.

PART 2: BE POLITE
SUGGESTIONS FOR DISCUSSION/FOLLOW-UP ACTIVITIES

- Discuss 'appropriate' forms of address, especially in a work context - to managers, to other employees.
- Consider how the head teacher has introduced the supermarket manager to the students - "Mr Brown".
- Consider formal and informal modes of address and discuss with students how they should decide which form of address is appropriate.
- Stress the importance of smiling, eye-contact and positive body language.
- Consider concepts of "familiarity" and "cheekiness" if appropriate.
- Mention why adults vary in the way they like to be addressed.
- Mention different factors (if appropriate), for example "respect", age difference, how well you know people, their positions, what they are taught.
- Mention school-by-school differences. For example the way students are taught to address their teaching assistants, minibus 'escorts', caretakers or dinner ladies.
- Stress the importance of getting into the habit of using the polite and respectful forms: "Please", "Thank you", "Sorry" "Excuse me" in everyday conversation. Also positive body language. Discuss how these devices cancel out small social 'gaffes' over first-names or surnames.

PART 3: BE HELPFUL
SUGGESTIONS FOR DISCUSSION/FOLLOW-UP ACTIVITIES

- Discuss how things can go wrong, even though the intentions are good.
- Discuss the importance of respecting other people's belongings, especially things they value.
- Consider, if appropriate, the mum's remark "You're a big help, you are!" – her tone of voice, likely facial expression and body language. Also look at other examples of irony or sarcasm: "Well, thank you very much!" (when the speaker doesn't really mean 'thank you') or "Well done! That's brilliant!" (when someone has obviously not been successful).
- Discuss with students how they can be "too helpful"; how they should finish one job before they start another etc.
- Discuss, with the students, when they should do what they're told on work experience, when they need to ask if they're not sure what to do, and when they can safely use their initiative.
- Consider situations when Philip might have been wrong to have cleared up the spilt milk, for example if the spillage involved broken glass or bleach (Health & Safety), or if he was in the middle of doing an important job for Donna.

Resources for: 'A Supermarket'

2. 'BAG PACKING' INTERACTIVE ACTIVITY TEACHER NOTES

RELATES TO: 'A SUPERMARKET' PAGES 18-19

(The four 'sorting' exercises are graded. It is advisable that students tackle them in order.)

OBJECTIVES

- Students gain an understanding of some basic principles of sorting shopping items and packing a shopping bag.
- Improve sorting and classifying skills.
- Improve their reading of labels on essential goods.

FEATURES

- 30 different shopping items appear randomly, though only 15 items come along the belt in any one exercise. If the student wants to play a game a second or third time, some of the items and the order in which they appear will change.
- Clicking on the tick box marked "Flags" will help the student to decide which items are "heavy & hard", "soft & breakable", or "smelly".

FOLLOW-UP ACTIVITIES

- Discuss with students if they pack their bags differently. If so, how?
- Ask students how they would apply these principles in 'real-life' shopping.

GET STARTED!

In this first part of the activity, students are invited to pack their shopping bags in any way they choose. This allows them a chance to work out what to do and sets up the next activity where students are asked to apply the first principle of bag packing – to avoid crushing the soft, breakable items.

DON'T SQUASH IT!

The student is now asked to separate just two types of shopping item:

1) Soft and breakable, and

2) Hard and heavy

There are several options open to the student: eg using up to five bags; keeping the two categories totally apart; putting some of the soft or breakable items on top of the hard, heavy ones.

NOT TOO HEAVY!

In this part, there are still only the previous two categories of item to deal with, but the student is also asked to think about the *weight* of the bags. Only four heavy items are allowed in a single bag.

HEAVY, SOFT OR SMELLY

In this part, there are three different types of shopping item for the student to deal with, with smelly items (for example, soap or washing powder) a fourth consideration.

3. 'SELL-BY DATES' INTERACTIVE ACTIVITY TEACHER NOTES

> **RELATES TO: 'A SUPERMARKET' PAGES 12-13**
>
> **LEVEL: 1-2**
>
> (The activities are graded, starting with the easiest.)
>
> ## OBJECTIVES
>
> - To prepare students for work experience in shops/supermarkets.
> - To increase awareness of time and an understanding of dates when arranged in different ways.
> - To increase the students' awareness of information on food packaging.
> - To improve students' sorting skills.
>
> NB: Not included: the "eat-by" date or the "best-before" date.
>
> ## FOLLOW-UP ACTIVITIES
>
> - Check food cupboards at home for items past their sell-by dates.
> - Discuss and clarify the terms "eat-by" and "best before".
> - Visit a food shop or supermarket and check sell-by dates before purchasing.
>
> ## OTHER POINTS
>
> - The year in each sell-by date is "live" and will update itself automatically so that it is always a date in the future.
> - Each game can be played several times because the different features (the food items for sorting, the months and so on) will alter automatically.

4. 'SIGNS AND AISLES' INTERACTIVE ACTIVITY TEACHER NOTES

RELATES TO: 'A SUPERMARKET' PAGES 6-7

LEVEL: 1-2

(The activities are graded, starting with the easiest.)

OBJECTIVES

- To learn more about the layout of a supermarket and the arrangement of goods.
- To increase sight-vocabulary of familiar items and categories through signs and flashcards.
- To improve grouping/sorting skills.

FOLLOW-UP ACTIVITIES

- A trip to the local supermarket to record the words on each aisle sign and how they are grouped together.
- Clarifying what the signs say and what the harder categories mean.
- Make signs for the classroom and practise putting them in groups.
- Role play in pairs, taking it in turns to be
    - A customer looking for a particular item, and
    - A student on work experience who has to help the customer to find it.

RESOURCE SHEETS FOR THE STUDENT

You may copy these sheets freely for use in your school.

There are seven resource sheets which relate specifically to *A Supermarket:*

1. HOW WELL DID YOU READ?
Ten simple true or false questions related to the text.

2. KEYWORD FLASHCARDS
Sixteen work-related words taken from the text. These need to be printed onto card and cut up.

3. WORDSEARCH
Ten key words chosen from the sixteen flashcards.

4. SPOT THE DIFFERENCE
An illustration from the book with six details changed.

5. THE BOOK AND ACTIVITIES: WHAT I THOUGHT OF THEM
Students write a sentence or two giving their views on the book and activities they've just tackled and think about anything they might have learned.

6. HOW WELL DID PHILIP DO?
Students look at Philip from Donna's point of view, and fill in a form about his attitude and performance.

7. STUDENT'S RECORD SHEET
A record sheet for the teacher to record the various activities undertaken by the student in this part of the course, and the level achieved.

There are also these additional sheets for the Work Experience course as a whole:

A. DETAILS OF MY PLACEMENT
A form or checklist for the student to fill in *before* his/her placement begins. It brings together all the main information the student will need.

B. MY WORK EXPERIENCE: HOW I GOT ON
An evaluation form students will complete *after* their placement. It will give them an opportunity to say how they got on, what they learned, and what they liked or didn't like.

Work Experience: A Supermarket

How well did you read?

Five of these are TRUE, and five are FALSE.

1. Philip did his work experience at a Premier supermarket. TRUE / FALSE

2. He did it for one week. TRUE / FALSE

3. He wore a uniform. TRUE / FALSE

4. His supervisor was called Elaine. TRUE / FALSE

5. Donna showed him the staffroom. TRUE / FALSE

6. All the aisles had numbers. TRUE / FALSE

7. He had a 20 minute break at 10.30. TRUE / FALSE

8. A customer asked him where the bacon was. TRUE / FALSE

9. A woman left a jar of coffee at the checkout. TRUE / FALSE

10. Philip's friends came to see him on Wednesday. TRUE / FALSE

© SEN Press 2007. All rights reserved.

Key words flashcards

aisle	break
checkout	customer
shelves	signs
stacked	store

© SEN Press 2007. All rights reserved.

Work Experience: A Supermarket

Key words flashcards

supermarket	work
uniform	lunch
notice	pack
toilets	staffroom

© SEN Press 2007. All rights reserved.

Spot the difference

Can you spot the six differences in the pictures? Ring them on the picture on the right.

Work Experience: A Supermarket

Work Experience: A Supermarket

The book and activities feedback sheet

1. Say what you thought of the book.
(Could you read it and understand it? Did you find it interesting? A bit? Was it boring? Did you like any of the illustrations? Which one(s)?)

....

....

....

2. Say what you thought of the interactive activities.
(Did you find them easy to use? Did you enjoy any of them? Which one(s)?)

....

....

....

3. Say if you learned anything from either.

....

....

....

....

© SEN Press 2007. All rights reserved.

How well did Philip do?

Imagine you are Donna filling in a form about Philip. How do you think she would answer these questions?

1.	Was Philip smartly dressed for work?	Yes/No
2.	Was he polite to customers?	Yes/No
3.	Was he good at stacking the shelves?	Yes/No
4.	Was he a good worker?	Yes/No
5.	Did he have the right attitude?	Yes/No
6.	Did you have to tick him off for any reason?	Yes/No

If "Yes", say what it was for:

....

....

....

Other comments:

....

....

....

....

© SEN Press 2007. All rights reserved.

Work Experience: A Supermarket

Student record sheet

A Supermarket

………………………………………………………………………….has,

- Read the text - with help/without help
- Made a contribution to the discussion - yes/no
- Completed the *How well did you read?* exercise - with help/without help
  Score:…………………………
- Tackled the 16 flashcards and achieved this score:…………………
- Completed these interactive activities
  - Golden Rules
  - Bag packing
  - Signs & aisles
  - Sell-by dates

- Completed these research or follow-up activities:

  - ………………………………………………………………………………
  - ………………………………………………………………………………

- Completed these other resource sheets:
  - Wordsearch
  - Spot the difference
  - How well did Philip do?
  - Book and activities feedback sheet

- Any other achievements or lessons learned:………………………………

………………………………………………………………………………………

………………………………………………………………………………………

………………………………………………………………………………………

© SEN Press 2007. All rights reserved.

Resources for: 'A Supermarket'

The following two generic resource sheets are also relevant to this book.

Full size worksheets for copying can be found on pages 111-112 of this book.

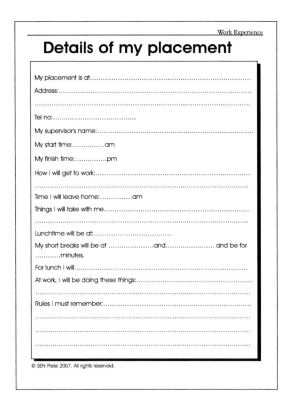

RESOURCES FOR 'A FAST-FOOD RESTAURANT'

'A FAST-FOOD RESTAURANT'

WORK EXPERIENCE SERIES

LEVEL: 1-2

READING AGE: 7.0 – 8.0 YEARS

24 PAGES

551 WORDS

KEY THEMES

Uniforms and personal appearance.

Independent travel.

Timekeeping.

Food hygiene.

A strict manageress.

Breaks and lunchtimes.

Other staff, customers.

Unpleasant jobs.

Coping with a mishap.

Joining in friendly staff banter.

THE NARRATIVE

The book features Suzanne, a strong personality, in a popular placement and a setting familiar to most (if not all) students. She is anxious to do well and please the manageress, and comes through several testing situations successfully. A collision with a customer, however, unsettles her and she wonders if this will be held against her.

This title covers many of the essential points that teachers will want to cover with their students.

More issues are touched on in the narrative, and teachers are given 'prompts' at the top corner of each right-hand page to remind them of points they could develop as they read through the book.

PAGE BY PAGE NOTES FOR THE TEACHER

A FAST-FOOD RESTAURANT: PAGE 1

- Discuss the key features in the illustration – the name on the awning, the drive-in sign, Suzanne's uniform etc.
- Ask related questions. Is there a fast-food restaurant near your school? Where? What is it called?
- Find out who has been there and when.
- Discuss what it might be like working there.

A FAST-FOOD RESTAURANT: PAGES 2-3

- Identify the different parts of Suzanne's uniform and what she is doing to it.
- Ask which students can iron clothes.
- Discuss why a uniform needs to be kept clean and shoes polished.
- What are the reasons for uniforms? (see 'What to Wear' Interactive Activity - page 25.)

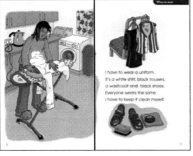

A FAST-FOOD RESTAURANT: PAGES 4-5

- Discuss different ways of travelling to work.
- The importance of punctuality. (See also the 'Golden Rules' Interactive Activity - page 6.)
- Where to sit: upstairs or downstairs?
- What to remember to take with you.

A FAST-FOOD RESTAURANT: PAGES 6-7

- Ask why hygiene in the kitchen is important - see 'Hygiene' Interactive Activity - see page 27.
- See also the 'Signs and Aisles' Interactive Activity - page 10.
- Why a manager has to be strict.

Resources for: 'A Fast-Food Restaurant'

A FAST-FOOD RESTAURANT: PAGES 8-9

- Talk about breaks - how long they're for, meeting other staff, what to do at these times.
- How to cope with staff who ignore you - see 'The Working Day' Interactive Activity - page 26.

A FAST-FOOD RESTAURANT: PAGES 10-11

- Talk about working in a busy environment.
- The need to be quick and efficient.
- Responding to firm but polite language and not taking offence.
- How to cope with rude customers.
- The consequences of 'answering back'.
- Responding to firm but polite language and not taking offence.

A FAST-FOOD RESTAURANT: PAGES 12-13

- Explore what to do if instructions aren't clear and students aren't sure what to do.
- Finding the confidence to ask.

A FAST-FOOD RESTAURANT: PAGES 14-15

- Talk about lunchtimes when students feel most isolated and awkward.
- How best to pass the time.
- Ways of joining in conversation - see 'The Working Day' Interactive Activity - page 26.
- Healthy and unhealthy food choices.

A FAST-FOOD RESTAURANT: PAGES 16-17

- Stress the importance of being flexible and helpful.
- Being prepared to do unpleasant jobs.
- Coping with things you don't like doing.

Resources for: 'A Fast-Food Restaurant'

A FAST-FOOD RESTAURANT: PAGES 18-19

- Mention busy times when it's easy to lose concentration & make mistakes.
- Look at the inside of the restaurant.
- Discuss the meals and prices on the large menu boards.
- Ask students which meal they would choose.

A FAST-FOOD RESTAURANT: PAGES 20-21

- Talk about the accident and what caused it:
  - how Suzanne will be feeling
  - what needs to be done
  - how serious it is
  - what Karen is likely to be thinking
  - coping with criticism.

A FAST-FOOD RESTAURANT: PAGES 22-23

- Talk about the end of Suzanne's day
  - when the other staff will be going home,
  - when the restaurant will close.
- Friendly staff banter and the importance of staying cheerful.

A FAST-FOOD RESTAURANT: PAGE 24

- Evaluate Suzanne's performance (see the Resource Sheet 'How Well Did Suzanne Do?' - page 34.)
- Discuss Suzanne and her qualities and if she was suitable for the job.
- What students think of the job and if they'd like to work there.
- Which parts of the job appeal most, or don't appeal at all.
- What they think of Karen.
- The qualities which are needed to make a success of a work placement.

Resources for: 'A Fast-Food Restaurant'

INTERACTIVE ACTIVITIES

There are three Interactive Activities that develop key themes in the narrative. Like all the Interactive Acitivies in this course they are designed for use both on whiteboards and individual PCs.

1. 'WHAT TO WEAR'

Suzanne is given a uniform to wear and to keep clean. This activity gets students thinking about the clothes that are worn in a number of different jobs, and the reasons behind particular choices. They also consider what might be appropriate/inappropriate, practical/impractical for their own placements.

See page 25 for full details of this Interactive Activity.

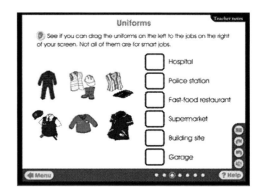

2. 'THE WORKING DAY'

The book mentions Suzanne's start and finish times, and her breaks and lunchtimes. This activity gets students to think about the structure of a typical working day, and the pattern of breaks adopted in most work places. They are asked to recognise time and make small time calculations using both analogue and digital clockfaces.

See page 26 for full details of this Interactive Activity.

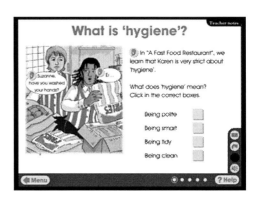

3. 'HYGIENE'

Suzanne is reminded to wash her hands while handling food in the kitchen. This activity looks at hygiene at work and at home, personal hygiene and the reasons for maintaining it. Students are asked to identify which work places and which parts of the house would require the strictest hygiene, and which cleaning agents are needed to achieve this. Students are also asked to consider their personal hygiene in a similar way.

See page 27 for full details of this Interactive Activity.

1. 'WHAT TO WEAR' INTERACTIVE ACTIVITY TEACHER NOTES

RELATES TO: 'A FAST-FOOD RESTAURANT' PAGES 2-3
LEVEL: 1-2

OBJECTIVES

Students consider:

- The reasons for different types of work clothing - for jobs with uniforms.
  - clean and dirty work
  - indoor and outdoor work
  - work requiring more subtle choices, between *smart* and *casual.*
- What *they* might be wearing on their work experience and why.
- If they like uniforms and consider them to be 'smart'.
- A range of possible placements, and the clothes they might be required to wear.
- Practicalities : clothes for cold and wet weather, jackets with fluorescent strips for road safety, footwear suitable for different conditions.
- Which jobs they like the look of, how they see themselves in particular clothes and which jobs they may be eligible for.

FOLLOW-UP ACTIVITIES

- Students list adults they know (friends, neighbours, relatives) and the jobs they do, and find out what clothes they wear to work.
- On school trips out and about (or even within the school itself), students record adults at work and the different clothes they wear, and discuss findings when they get back to school.

2. 'THE WORKING DAY' INTERACTIVE ACTIVITY TEACHER NOTES

RELATES TO: 'A FAST-FOOD RESTAURANT' PAGES 4, 9, 14, 22

LEVEL: 1-2

OBJECTIVES

Students learn about:

- The breakdown of a normal working day.
- Key times on clockfaces.
- Analogue and digital clock faces.
- Lengths of normal breaks and lunchtimes.
- When ¼ hour and 1 hour breaks will finish.

FOLLOW-UP ACTIVITIES

Help students prepare for their own work experience:

- Learn the key times in their working day.
- Learn about the breaktimes and lunchtimes at their places of work.
- Make sure they are clear about eating arrangements at work – if there is a canteen, or a staffroom, if people bring their own sandwiches and drink, where to sit etc.
- Know how to pass the time (breaks and lunchtimes).
- Role play – different situations involving hygiene.

3. 'HYGIENE'
INTERACTIVE ACTIVITY TEACHER NOTES

RELATES TO: 'A FAST-FOOD RESTAURANT' PAGES 6-7
LEVEL: 1-2

OBJECTIVES

Students learn about:
(reinforcement)
- The meaning of the term.
- Achieving personal hygiene.
- Achieving hygiene in the home and at work.
- Appropriate cleaning agents for home and work.
- Workplaces requiring the strictest hygiene.

FOLLOW-UP ACTIVITIES

Further discussion of:
- Personal hygiene – where to wash, when, how often, with what etc.
- Washing agents – what they achieve, why we use them.
- Keeping clothes clean.
- Bacteria: keeping the kitchen, the toilets hygienic.

Role-play of similar situations.

Resources for: 'A Fast-Food Restaurant'

RESOURCE SHEETS FOR THE STUDENT

You may copy these sheets freely for use in your school.

There are seven resource sheets which relate specifically to *A Fast-Food Restaurant*:

1. HOW WELL DID YOU READ?

Ten simple true or false questions related to the text.

2. KEYWORD FLASHCARDS

16 work-related words taken from the text. These need to be printed onto card and cut up.

3. WORDSEARCH

Ten key words chosen from the 16 flashcards.

4. SPOT THE DIFFERENCE

An illustration from the book with six details changed.

5. THE BOOK AND ACTIVITIES: WHAT I THOUGHT OF THEM

Students write a sentence or two giving their views on the book and activities they've just tackled and think about anything they might have learned.

6. HOW WELL DID SUZANNE DO?

Students look at Suzanne from Karen's point of view, and fill in a form about her attitude and performance.

7. STUDENT'S RECORD SHEET

A record sheet for the teacher to record the various activities undertaken by the student in this part of the course, and the level achieved.

There are also these additional sheets for the Work Experience course as a whole:

A. DETAILS OF MY PLACEMENT

A form or checklist for the student to fill in *before* his/her placement begins. It brings together all the main information the student will need.

B. MY WORK EXPERIENCE: HOW I GOT ON

An evaluation form students will complete *after* their placement. It will give them an opportunity to say how they got on, what they learned, and what they liked or didn't like.

Work Experience: A Fast-Food Restaurant

How well did you read?

Five of these are TRUE, and five are FALSE.

1. Suzanne worked two days a week.	TRUE / FALSE
2. Her mum washed and ironed her uniform.	TRUE / FALSE
3. She travelled to work by bus.	TRUE / FALSE
4. She started work at 9 o'clock.	TRUE / FALSE
5. Her boss was called Karen.	TRUE / FALSE
6. The rude customer wanted Suzanne to bring a cloth.	TRUE / FALSE
7. Suzanne was asked to sweep up outside.	TRUE / FALSE
8. Suzanne dropped a bottle of coke on the ground.	TRUE / FALSE
9. She finished work at 4 o'clock.	TRUE / FALSE
10. A burger cost £1.60.	TRUE / FALSE

© SEN Press 2007. All rights reserved.

Key words flashcards

restaurant	work
uniform	bus
hygiene	staff
lunch	telephone

© SEN Press 2007. All rights reserved.

Key words flashcards

clean	customer
minutes	o'clock
late	break
people	busy

Work Experience: A Fast-Food Restaurant

Wordsearch

Search for the hidden words from the lists in this grid.

r	e	s	t	a	u	r	a	n	t	a	c
d	z	n	e	g	c	p	k	r	m	h	u
c	l	e	a	n	g	x	s	c	l	y	s
i	j	m	u	y	f	g	p	q	u	g	t
w	e	n	q	a	k	e	u	b	n	i	o
o	f	a	s	t	a	f	f	a	c	e	m
r	v	e	a	t	s	n	h	c	h	n	e
k	n	s	v	y	j	u	g	a	o	e	r
a	c	f	b	u	s	a	d	i	r	l	p
m	t	e	l	e	p	h	o	n	e	q	a
f	a	j	h	c	x	u	l	k	a	l	r
u	n	i	f	o	r	m	u	h	e	c	a

restaurant   staff
work   lunch
uniform   telephone
bus   clean
hygiene   customer

© SEN Press 2007. All rights reserved.

32

Work Experience: A Fast-Food Restaurant

Spot the difference

Can you spot the six differences in the pictures? Ring them on the picture on the right.

Work Experience: A Fast-Food Restaurant

The book and activities feedback sheet

1. Say what you thought of the book.
(Could you read it and understand it? Did you find it interesting? A bit? Was it boring? Did you like any of the illustrations? Which one(s)?)

....

....

....

2. Say what you thought of the interactive activities.
(Did you find them easy to use? Did you enjoy any of them? Which one(s)?)

....

....

....

3. Say if you learned anything from either.

....

....

....

....

© SEN Press 2007. All rights reserved.

Work Experience: A Fast-Food Restaurant

How well did Suzanne do?

Imagine you are Karen filling in a form about Suzanne. How do you think she would answer these questions?

1. Did she keep her uniform clean?   Yes/No

2. Was she polite to customers?   Yes/No

3. Did she get on with the other staff?   Yes/No

4. Did she work hard?   Yes/No

5. Did she have the right attitude?   Yes/No

6. Did you have to tick her off for any reason?   Yes/No

If "Yes", say what it was for:

....

....

....

Other comments:

....

....

....

....

© SEN Press 2007. All rights reserved.

Student record sheet
A Fast-Food Restaurant

....has,

- Read the text - with help/without help
- Made a contribution to the discussion - yes/no
- Completed the *How well did you read?* exercise - with help/without help Score:...........................
- Tackled the 16 flashcards and achieved this score:....................
- Completed these interactive activities
    - What to wear
    - The working day
    - Hygiene

- Completed these research or follow-up activities:

    - ....
    - ....

- Completed these other resource sheets:
    - Wordsearch
    - Spot the difference
    - How well did Suzanne do?
    - Book and activities feedback sheet

- Any other achievements or lessons learned:...................................

....
....
....

© SEN Press 2007. All rights reserved.

Resources for: 'A Fast-Food Restaurant'

The following two generic resource sheets are also relevant to this book.

Full size worksheets for copying can be found on pages 111-112 of this book.

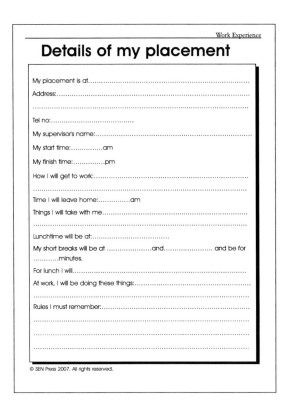

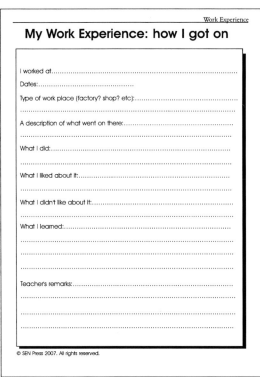

37

RESOURCES FOR 'A CHARITY SHOP'

'A CHARITY SHOP'

WORK EXPERIENCE SERIES

LEVEL: 1-2

READING AGE: 7.0 – 8.0 YEARS

24 PAGES

580 WORDS

KEY THEMES

Tiredness from work.

Getting to know other staff and problems remembering their names.

Sorting and classifying skills (clothes sizes).

Concentration on the job.

An accident with a steamer, first aid.

Recycling unwanted goods.

Learning assertiveness.

Opportunities for showing initiative.

THE NARRATIVE

The story features Lisa, a quiet girl with little obvious self-confidence. She suffers many of the difficulties felt by students on work experience for the first time – a long day, tiredness, not knowing anyone, forgetting names of other staff – but she tries hard and succeeds in sympathetic surroundings.

Woven into the narrative are examples of the varied work offered by charity shops, both behind the scenes and in the shop itself. In a scene towards the end, Lisa learns that she has an effective voice when two customers knowingly block her way and show no sign of moving.

More topics are touched on in the narrative, and teachers are given 'prompts' at the top corner of each right-hand page to remind them of points they could develop as they read through the book.

PAGE BY PAGE NOTES FOR THE TEACHER

A CHARITY SHOP: PAGE 1

- Ask students about charity shops: if there are any in town; what they're called, what they sell; where the goods come from; if any of the students have been in one.
- How do students view them? Is there any stigma attached? Should they be valued for recycling our unwanted household goods?
- Lisa and her appearance.

A CHARITY SHOP: PAGES 2-3

- Consider Lisa's observations about working in the shop.
- Her concerns.
- The tiredness she feels.
- The hours (9.00 – 4.30) may be longer than many students will be expected to work.

A CHARITY SHOP: PAGES 4-5

- Talk about introductions and remembering names.
- Volunteer staff of charity shops working on different days.
- Lisa's likely feelings at first.

A CHARITY SHOP: PAGES 6-7

- Quiz students about clothes labels – what information they provide. (See 'Labels & Sorting' Interactive Activity - page 45.)
- What do students know about their own sizes?
- How clothes are displayed in shops.
- The last time students were in a clothes shop.
- What they bought.
- Trying on clothes before you buy.

Resources for: 'A Charity Shop'

A CHARITY SHOP: PAGES 8-9

- Establish what a 'steamer' is, what it does, and how it differs from an iron.
- The risks in using a steamer.
- What Lisa is doing wrong.

A CHARITY SHOP: PAGES 10-11

- First aid. See the 'Health & Safety' Interactive Activity - page 43 - and the section looking at first aid and the contents of a first aid box.
- Students' experiences of burns or scalds and how they were treated.

A CHARITY SHOP: PAGES 12-13

- Think of all the different things that may need sorting in a charity shop.
- The expression "daft as a brush" and other other expressions older people use.
- Things that make us laugh.

A CHARITY SHOP: PAGES 14-15

- Talk about things we throw away and what happens to them.
- Recycling and home collections.
- The importance of taking care with lifting and not being 'macho'.
- How to lift things properly and how our backs are designed.

A CHARITY SHOP: PAGES 16-17

- Focus on Billy and his likely age.
- The temptation to chat with people of your own age when you should be working.

Resources for: 'A Charity Shop'

A CHARITY SHOP: PAGES 18-19

- Think about customers who are inconsiderate.
- How to control feelings and stay polite at all times.
- How to say the right thing in the right way (see 'Dealing with Customers' Interactive Activity - page 44.).

A CHARITY SHOP: PAGES 20-21

- Think of situations when you think something may be wrong and you feel you ought to say something.
- Think about what "using your initiative" means and its place in work experience.

A CHARITY SHOP: PAGES 22-23

- Think about how we can show our appreciation of others.
- How we feel (shy, embarrassed, proud etc) when we are praised in front of others.

A CHARITY SHOP: PAGE 24

- Evaluate Lisa's performance (see Resource Sheet 'How well did Lisa do?' - page 53).
- Discuss Lisa and her qualities and if she was suitable for the job.
- What students think of the job and if they would like to work there.
- Which parts of the job appeal most? And least?

Resources for: 'A Charity Shop'

INTERACTIVE ACTIVITIES

There are three interactive activities that develop key themes in the narrative. They are designed for use both on whiteboards and individual PCs.

1. HEALTH & SAFETY

This activity relates to Lisa's accident with a steamer. It deals with situations from all six Work Experience titles, not just *A Charity Shop*. Students look at lifting heavy boxes (*A Supermarket*); handling animals (*An Animal Charity*); machinery (*An Interview*) and so on.

They also take a look at First Aid and the contents of a typical First Aid Box. They are asked to think about a range of injuries, some serious requiring hospital treatment, others mere scratches or grazes treatable with a First Aid Box.

See page 43 for full details of this Interactive Activity.

2. DEALING WITH CUSTOMERS

This activity relates to Lisa dealing with the women blocking her way.

It looks at the student working in the shop and having to deal with a number of different situations involving customers. Students are also asked to consider the maxim: "The customer is always right."

See page 44 for full details of this Interactive Activity.

3. LABELS AND SORTING

This activity relates to Lisa sorting clothes on hangers according to their label size.

Students consider the information given on clothes labels, both size labels (women's and men's) and care labels.

The activities test their ability to arrange clothes on hangers in size order, and to recognise care symbols for washing and ironing purposes.

See page 45 for full details of this Interactive Activity.

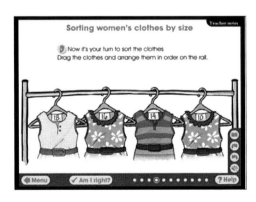

1. 'HEALTH & SAFETY' INTERACTIVE ACTIVITY TEACHER NOTES

RELATES TO: 'A CHARITY SHOP' PAGES 10-11
LEVEL: 1-2

OBJECTIVES

- Students look at a number of Health & Safety issues from the Work Experience series and learn to identify some of the risks:
  - incorrect lifting
  - animal handling
  - heavy machinery
  - slippery floors
  - burns and scalds.

- Students consider First Aid:
  - a First Aid Box and what it contains
  - distinguishing between accidents that require (a) First Aid only and (b) hospital/clinic treatment.

FOLLOW-UP ACTIVITIES

- Look at Health & Safety at school, at home, in public places (eg a cinema, a shopping centre)
  - consider fire exits and fire drills
  - examine with individual students the Health & Safety issues on their work placements
  - role play – accidents and appropriate treatments.

2. 'DEALING WITH CUSTOMERS' INTERACTIVE ACTIVITY TEACHER NOTES

RELATES TO: 'A CHARITY SHOP' PAGES 18-19
LEVEL: 1-2

OBJECTIVES

- Students learn four important lessons for work experience:
  - to ask for help if customers ask them questions they can't answer
  - to be prepared for a few ill-mannered customers
  - the maxim "The customer is always right"
  - how they should try to be polite at all times.

NB Students who are going to work in a shop will need to know how much time is likely to be spent 'behind the scenes' and how much in the shop itself. They should understand that they will probably not be expected to serve customers by themselves, and certainly not handle customers' money without help.

FOLLOW-UP ACTIVITIES

- Further discussion on 'the customer is always right', what it means and why shops go to great lengths to keep their customers.
- Further discussion on self-assertiveness, and how to say what you want without giving offence.
- Role play – either the situations presented in the book or different ones requiring the student to be polite to customers.

3. 'LABELS AND SORTING' INTERACTIVE ACTIVITY TEACHER NOTES

RELATES TO: 'A CHARITY SHOP' PAGES 6-7

LEVEL: 1-3

Warning
The first activity deals with the subject of size which will need to be dealt with sensitively.

OBJECTIVES

Students learn about:

- Clothes handling in a charity shop or clothes shop.
- The information given on clothes labels.
- Clothes sizes and how they are arranged on racks.
- Clothes care information on labels – washing, drying, ironing etc.
- The symbols and their meaning.
- General sorting skills.

FOLLOW-UP ACTIVITIES

- Students measure and record their own personal sizes and measurements.
- Make visits to a men's clothes shop, a women's clothes shop, a supermarket.
- Identify and learn about different clothes materials and how each should be handled.
- Discuss some of the accidents that have occurred when people have ignored important warning labels.
- Role play (a shop setting: conversation between customer and sales staff, discussion about sizes, measurements etc).

Resources for: 'A Charity Shop'

RESOURCE SHEETS FOR THE STUDENT

You may copy these sheets freely for use in your school.

There are seven resource sheets which relate specifically to *A Charity Shop*:

1. HOW WELL DID YOU READ?

Ten simple true or false questions related to the text.

2. KEYWORD FLASHCARDS

Sixteen work-related words taken from the text. These need to be printed onto card and cut up.

3. WORDSEARCH

Ten key words chosen from the sixteen flashcards.

4. SPOT THE DIFFERENCE

An illustration from the book with six details changed.

5. THE BOOK AND ACTIVITIES: WHAT I THOUGHT OF THEM

Students write a sentence or two giving their views on the book and activities they've just tackled and think about anything they might have learned.

6. HOW WELL DID LISA DO?

Students look at Lisa from Margaret's point of view, and fill in a form about her attitude and performance.

7. STUDENT'S RECORD SHEET

A record sheet for the teacher to record the various activities undertaken by the student in this part of the course, and the level achieved.

There are also these additional sheets for the Work Experience course as a whole:

A. DETAILS OF MY PLACEMENT

A form or checklist for the student to fill in *before* his/her placement begins. It brings together all the main information the student will need.

B. MY WORK EXPERIENCE: HOW I GOT ON

An evaluation form students will complete *after* their placement. It will give them an opportunity to say how they got on, what they learned, and what they liked or didn't like.

How well did you read?

Work Experience: A Charity Shop

Five of these are TRUE, and five are FALSE.

1. The student's name was Lisa.	TRUE / FALSE
2. The manager's name was Billy.	TRUE / FALSE
3. Lisa had an accident with a steamer.	TRUE / FALSE
4. Margaret rang for the ambulance.	TRUE / FALSE
5. Lisa had to go to the hospital.	TRUE / FALSE
6. Billy went to fetch some cold water.	TRUE / FALSE
7. There were some big recycling bins at the back.	TRUE / FALSE
8. Lisa found a woman's ring in a jacket.	TRUE / FALSE
9. A woman gave Lisa a box of chocolates.	TRUE / FALSE
10. Lisa worked in the shop for a week.	TRUE / FALSE

© SEN Press 2007. All rights reserved.

Key words flashcards

charity	shop
manager	label
size	washing
iron	clothes

Work Experience: A Charity Shop

Key words flashcards

message	morning
accident	wrong
temperature	dry
shirt	First-Aid

© SEN Press 2007. All rights reserved.

Wordsearch

Work Experience: A Charity Shop

Search for the hidden words from the lists in this grid.

c	h	a	r	i	t	y	a	c	m	a	c
d	e	n	e	g	c	k	o	e	o	h	u
c	l	a	b	e	l	x	s	r	r	y	s
i	j	m	d	y	f	g	p	l	n	g	h
m	e	s	s	a	g	e	f	n	i	i	o
o	f	a	s	i	z	e	f	a	n	c	p
y	v	e	h	o	a	r	k	c	g	l	w
m	k	s	v	h	j	u	l	a	o	o	r
a	c	f	q	u	s	a	r	i	r	t	p
w	a	s	h	i	n	g	o	r	e	h	e
f	a	j	h	l	x	u	l	o	a	e	v
m	a	n	a	g	e	r	v	n	e	s	o

charity   washing
shop   iron
manager   clothes
label   message
size   morning

© SEN Press 2007. All rights reserved.

Spot the difference

Can you spot the six differences in the pictures? Ring them on the picture on the right.

Work Experience: A Charity Shop

Work Experience: A Charity Shop

The book and activities feedback sheet

1. Say what you thought of the book.
(Could you read it and understand it? Did you find it interesting? A bit? Was it boring? Did you like any of the illustrations? Which one(s)?)

....

....

....

2. Say what you thought of the interactive activities.
(Did you find them easy to use? Did you enjoy any of them? Which one(s)?)

....

....

....

3. Say if you learned anything from either.

....

....

....

....

© SEN Press 2007. All rights reserved.

Work Experience: A Charity Shop

How well did Lisa do?

Imagine you are Margaret filling in a form about Lisa. How do you think she would answer these questions?

1.	Was Lisa smart enough?	Yes/No
2.	Was she polite?	Yes/No
3.	Did she get on with other staff?	Yes/No
4.	Did she try hard?	Yes/No
5.	Did she have the right attitude?	Yes/No
6.	Did you have to tick her off for any reason?	Yes/No

If "Yes", say what it was for:

....

....

....

Other comments:

....

....

....

....

© SEN Press 2007. All rights reserved.

Work Experience: A Charity Shop

Student record sheet

A Charity Shop

....has,

- Read the text - with help/without help
- Made a contribution to the discussion - yes/no
- Completed the *How well did you read*? exercise - with help/without help
  Score:...............................
- Tackled the 16 flashcards and achieved this score:....................
- Completed these interactive activities
    - Health and safety
    - Dealing with customers
    - Labels and sorting

- Completed these research or follow-up activities:

    - ....
    - ....

- Completed these other resource sheets:
    - Wordsearch
    - Spot the difference
    - How well did Lisa do?
    - Book and activities feedback sheet

- Any other achievements or lessons learned:....................................

....

....

....

....

© SEN Press 2007. All rights reserved.

Resources for: 'A Charity Shop'

The following two generic resource sheets are also relevant to this book.

Full size worksheets for copying can be found on pages 111-112 of this book.

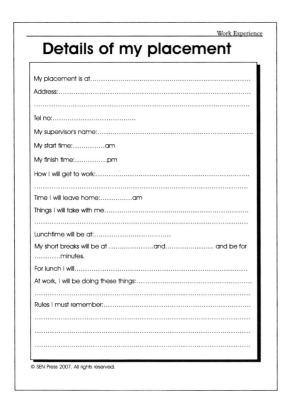

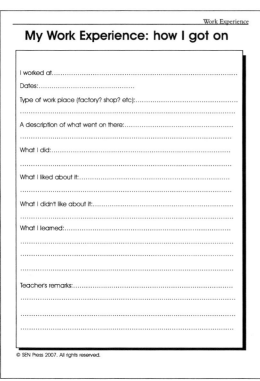

RESOURCES FOR 'A GARAGE'

'A GARAGE'

WORK EXPERIENCE SERIES

LEVEL: 1-2

READING AGE: 7.0 – 8.0 YEARS

24 PAGES

460 WORDS

KEY THEMES

How not to behave on work experience.

The purpose of work experience.

Unrealistic student expectations.

Right and wrong student attitudes.

Punctuality and lateness.

Learning by observing.

Skills and qualifications.

Willingness.

The employer's point of view, and his responsibility to his customers.

Risks to safety.

THE NARRATIVE

Wayne is an unmitigated disaster on his work experience. The story gives teachers an opportunity to cover all the things *not to do*, to discuss the problem of false expectations and arriving on a placement with the wrong attitude to work. They can also point to bad behaviour not being tolerated in the workplace and make students aware of the need for training and qualifications in this kind of work. Students meet Mr Potts, a strict employer, who won't put up with unsatisfactory behaviour or a reluctance to learn, and Wayne's work experience lasts only one day.

Students also get an opportunity to see things through Mr Potts' eyes and consider what work experience is really for.

More topics are touched on in the narrative, and teachers are given 'prompts' at the top corner of each right-hand page to remind them of points they could develop as they read through the book.

PAGE BY PAGE NOTES FOR THE TEACHER

A GARAGE: PAGE 1

- Talk about the brother's sports car. Would students like a car like this? Would it give them a thrill? Why?
- Do they think working in a garage would give them the same thrill? How would they feel about mending dirty old cars and vans?

A GARAGE: PAGES 2-3

- Ask the students what they think is happening in the picture. What do they think Wayne has been asked to do?
- Talk about the text. Does it tell us how Wayne is getting on?
- How many students have ever been to a garage?

A GARAGE: PAGES 4-5

- Discuss the importance of punctuality, especially on the first day.
- Discuss Wayne's excuse and the way he answers back.
- What should Wayne have said?

A GARAGE: PAGES 6-7

- Ask students to say why they think the overalls were bothering Wayne.
- What do they think he was wanting? Why? Was he right to have a moan?
- What would Mr Potts say?

Resources for: 'A Garage'

A GARAGE: PAGES 8-9

- Ask the students what they know about qualifications for being a car mechanic.
- Talk about Mr Potts. Is he being fussy?
- Should he be letting Wayne have a go at changing the brakes? What are brakes?

A GARAGE: PAGES 10-11

- Mr Potts asked Wayne to make the tea. Was this right?
- Wayne thought he was there to mend cars. Was he right to think this? What *is* work experience in a garage for?

A GARAGE: PAGES 12-13

- Talk about the tools used in a garage.
- What are their names? What are they for?
- Is it important to keep tools tidy? Why?
- What does the number plate of the red car tell us about the age of the car?

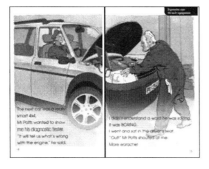

A GARAGE: PAGES 14-15

- Ask students to say what they think is happening (going wrong) in the picture.
- Is Mr Potts being fair? What do they think *he* would say?
- See 'The Employer's Point of View' Interactive Activity - page 61.
- Clarify what the term '4x4' means.

A GARAGE: PAGES 16-17

- Clarify the meaning of 'spare parts'.
- How does a garage get hold of spare parts?
- Where do they come from and how quickly are they delivered?

Resources for: 'A Garage'

A GARAGE: PAGES 18-19

- See 'Learning by Watching' Interactive Activity - page 63 - in which students are asked to watch the different stages of changing a wheel.
- Is Mr Potts right to do the job himself?
- What are the risks if he lets Wayne do it?

A GARAGE: PAGES 20-21

- Ask the students if they think Mr Potts is being fair.
- Recall all the small things that convince Mr Potts that having Wayne working at the garage isn't going to work.
- Should Wayne be given a second chance?

A GARAGE: PAGES 22-23

- What do students think Mr Parker will do?
- Is Mr Potts likely take any more students on work experience?

A GARAGE: PAGE 24

- Go through the list of questions on the evaluation form.
- Mention to the students that their employer will be filling in a form about them when they have finished work experience.
- Discuss what to say in "Other comments"

Resources for: 'A Garage'

INTERACTIVE ACTIVITIES

There are three interactive activities that develop key themes in the narrative. Like all the Interactive Activities in this course they are designed for use both on whiteboards and individual PCs.

1. THE EMPLOYER'S POINT OF VIEW

This activity relates to Mr Potts filling in the report form on Wayne. The student is given three simple cloze passages to complete, on different topics:

- How Mr Potts regards his job.
- How he views Wayne and work experience generally.

See page 61 for full details of this Interactive Activity.

2. WHAT TO EXPECT ON WORK EXPERIENCE

This activity relates to Wayne's assumption that he was there to mend cars). It introduces scenes from all six titles in the Work Experience reading books series.

Students consider eight "frequently asked questions" and have a go at answering them. Questions such as: "Will I be paid?" and "Will I be offered a proper job when I leave school?".

There are also questions on working practice: "Can I go to the toilet when I want?" and "What if I can't get to work on time?"

This activity is best directed by the teacher who can widen the discussion to include other issues that students aren't clear or happy about.

See page 62 for full details of this Interactive Activity.

3. LEARNING BY WATCHING

This activity relates to Wayne wanting to change a car wheel by himself. An essential part of work experience is learning through observation. In this activity, students observe Mr Potts changing a wheel on a car, through a sequence of illustrations. This is done is two stages

a) taking off the wheel that has the puncture and
b) putting on the spare tyre.

Students have to remember the sequence of actions, and recreate the sequence correctly.

See page 63 for full details of this Interactive Activity.

1. 'THE EMPLOYER'S POINT OF VIEW' INTERACTIVE ACTIVITY TEACHER NOTES

RELATES TO: 'A GARAGE' PAGES 5, 8, 9, 11, 14, 15, 17, 18, 22, 24

LEVEL: 1-2

OBJECTIVES

Students tackle three similar cloze activities requiring anticipation skills in their reading. They also learn that:

- Work experience isn't just about them.
- Employers have a responsibility to their customers.
- Some employers won't stand for any nonsense.
- They might be sent home if they don't do as they are asked.
- Their behaviour, punctuality and attitude will be monitored.

All these points need to be reinforced by the teacher.

NB Weaker readers will need help with completing the cloze passages.

FOLLOW-UP ACTIVITIES

- Discussion on businesses and how they work.
- Discussion on how students will fit into a busy working environment.
- Discussion on safety issues and risks in a garage or workshop.
- Role play situations (see teacher notes for the 'What to Expect on Work Experience' Interactive Activity - page 62).
- Students complete the second half of the employer's evaluation form Resource Sheet.

Resources for: 'A Garage'

2. 'WHAT TO EXPECT ON WORK EXPERIENCE' INTERACTIVE ACTIVITY TEACHER NOTES

> **RELATES TO: 'A GARAGE' PAGES 2, 5, 6, 8, 9, 11, 12, 14, 15, 17, 18, 21, 22, 24**
>
> **LEVEL: 1-2+**
>
> This is a key activity best directed by the teacher and not left to the student to tackle on his/her own. The questions have been kept deliberately simple, but they should be seen as a starting point for discussion on wider, harder issues.
>
> ### OBJECTIVES
>
> Students discuss and learn about:
>
> - The main purpose of work experience.
> - What they might expect to do on their placements.
> - The realistic chances of proper jobs afterwards - the limited opportunities open to them when they leave school/college.
> - Jobs requiring training and qualifications.
> - Paid and unpaid work.
> - A selection of important DOs and DON'Ts.
>
> ### FOLLOW-UP WORK
>
> - Students research their work experience placement more thoroughly, especially what they are likely to be doing, DOs and DON'Ts etc.
> - Students can assemble relevant details/findings using the 'Details of My Placement' Resource Sheet (see page 111).
> - Wider discussion on what work experience is for.
> - Talk about Wayne in the story: his 'attitude' and expectations.
> - Various role play situations involving Mr Potts struggling to get Wayne to do various simple tasks; Mr Potts telling Wayne why he doesn't want him back and so on.
> - Students consider and evaluate Wayne's performance - see the 'How Well did Wayne Do?' Resource Sheet (see page 71).

3. 'LEARNING BY WATCHING' INTERACTIVE ACTIVITY TEACHER NOTES

> **RELATES TO: 'A GARAGE' PAGES 18-19**
>
> **LEVEL: 1-2**
>
> (The activities are graded, starting with the easiest.)
>
> ## OBJECTIVES
>
> Students learn to:
>
> - Concentrate on a simple demonstration (changing the wheel on a car).
> - Repeat it themselves in two separate stages.
> - Show observation skills.
> - Recall a sequence of actions.
> - Make sense of what is happening (why the car needs to be on flat ground, etc).
>
> ## FOLLOW-UP ACTIVITIES
>
> - Safety: students discuss things that could have gone wrong if Wayne had been allowed to handle this by himself.
> - Students (and teacher) recall personal experiences of any punctures or breakdowns. (Where did they occur? Where were they going? How were they were mended? How long did it take?)
> - Students find out more about what people can do when their vehicles break down (eg a possible sequence of events, breakdown services like AA or RAC, breakdown vehicles, useful/ essential toolkits).
> - Role play: a vehicle breakdown (the sequence of events).

Resources for: 'A Garage'

RESOURCE SHEETS FOR THE STUDENT

You may copy these sheets freely for use in your school.

There are seven resource sheets which relate specifically to *A Garage:*

1. HOW WELL DID YOU READ?

Ten simple true or false questions related to the text.

2. KEYWORD FLASHCARDS

Sixteen work-related words taken from the text. These need to be printed onto card and cut up.

3. WORDSEARCH

Ten key words chosen from the sixteen flashcards.

4. SPOT THE DIFFERENCE

An illustration from the book with six details changed.

5. THE BOOK AND ACTIVITIES: WHAT I THOUGHT OF THEM

Students write a sentence or two giving their views on the book and activities they've just tackled and think about anything they might have learned.

6. HOW WELL DID WAYNE DO?

Students look at Wayne from Mr Potts' point of view, and fill in a form about his attitude and performance.

7. STUDENT'S RECORD SHEET

A record sheet for the teacher to record the various activities undertaken by the student in this part of the course, and the level achieved.

There are also these additional sheets for the Work Experience course as a whole:

A. DETAILS OF MY PLACEMENT

A form or checklist for the student to fill in *before* his/her placement begins. It brings together all the main information the student will need.

B. MY WORK EXPERIENCE: HOW I GOT ON

An evaluation form students will complete *after* their placement. It will give them an opportunity to say how they got on, what they learned, and what they liked or didn't like.

How well did you read?

Work Experience: A Garage

Five of these are TRUE, and five are FALSE.

1. Wayne's brother had a red sports car.	TRUE / FALSE
2. The owner of the garage was called Mr Potts.	TRUE / FALSE
3. Wayne was given clean overalls to wear.	TRUE / FALSE
4. He was asked to make the tea.	TRUE / FALSE
5. The spare parts were for the old van.	TRUE / FALSE
6. Wayne was told to mend the puncture.	TRUE / FALSE
7. Mr Potts said that Wayne's attitude was wrong.	TRUE / FALSE
8. Mr Potts e-mailed Mr Parker.	TRUE / FALSE
9. He didn't want Wayne to come back.	TRUE / FALSE
10. Wayne's surname was Rooney.	TRUE / FALSE

© SEN Press 2007. All rights reserved.

Key words flashcards

garage	late
overalls	van
brakes	kettle
engine	wheel

Key words flashcards

tyre	car
mend	fault
quick	safety
qualifications	tidy

Wordsearch

Work Experience: A Garage

Search for the hidden words from the lists in this grid.

l	h	b	r	a	k	e	s	d	n	p	w
f	j	r	m	b	f	a	u	x	k	e	h
p	q	y	n	l	v	a	n	k	e	d	e
h	c	o	u	e	a	h	m	l	t	u	e
g	a	r	a	g	e	b	k	r	t	t	l
w	v	l	q	k	p	d	h	t	l	g	f
z	t	y	r	e	d	r	p	u	e	l	b
c	r	y	e	q	t	i	a	r	o	a	s
e	n	g	i	n	e	a	i	b	d	t	e
d	r	a	w	i	n	g	o	l	e	e	r
n	k	b	c	a	r	i	g	u	s	q	x
o	v	e	r	a	l	l	s	s	b	d	h

garage   kettle
late   engine
overalls   wheel
van   tyre
brakes   car

© SEN Press 2007. All rights reserved.

Spot the difference

Can you spot the six differences in the pictures? Ring them on the picture on the right.

Work Experience: A Garage

69

Work Experience: A Garage

The book and activities feedback sheet

1. Say what you thought of the book.
(Could you read it and understand it? Did you find it interesting? A bit? Was it boring? Did you like any of the illustrations? Which one(s)?)

....

....

....

2. Say what you thought of the interactive activities.
(Did you find them easy to use? Did you enjoy any of them? Which one(s)?)

....

....

....

3. Say if you learned anything from either.

....

....

....

....

© SEN Press 2007. All rights reserved.

How well did Wayne do?

Imagine you are Mr Potts filling in a form about Wayne. How do you think he would answer these questions?

1.	Was he punctual?	Yes/No
2.	Did he do what he was asked?	Yes/No
3.	Did he try hard?	Yes/No
4.	Was he polite?	Yes/No
5.	Did he have the right attitude?	Yes/No
6.	Did you have to tick him off for any reason?	Yes/No

If "Yes", say what it was for:

....

....

....

Other comments:

....

....

....

....

… Work Experience: A Garage

Student record sheet
A Garage

....has,

- Read the text - with help/without help
- Made a contribution to the discussion - yes/no
- Completed the *How well did you read?* exercise - with help/without help
  Score:............................
- Tackled the 16 flashcards and achieved this score:....................
- Completed these interactive activities
  - The employer's point of view
  - What to expect
  - Learning by watching

- Completed these research or follow-up activities:

  - ....
  - ....

- Completed these other resource sheets:
  - Wordsearch
  - Spot the difference
  - How well did Wayne do?
  - Book and activities feedback sheet

- Any other achievements or lessons learned:......................................

....

....

....

© SEN Press 2007. All rights reserved.

Resources for: 'A Garage'

The following two generic resource sheets are also relevant to this book.

Full size worksheets for copying can be found on pages 111-112 of this book.

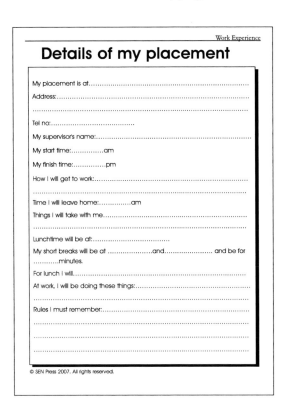

RESOURCES FOR 'AN ANIMAL CHARITY'

'AN ANIMAL CHARITY'

WORK EXPERIENCE SERIES

LEVEL: 1-2

READING AGE: 7.0 – 8.0 YEARS

24 PAGES

540 WORDS

KEY THEMES

Students arranging their own placements.

Interviews.

Seeing examples of animal cruelty.

Sickness and death.

Outdoor working conditions.

Routines.

Training and qualifications.

Voluntary unpaid work.

THE NARRATIVE

The book features Jessica, who wants to work in a local animal rescue centre although she knows her chance of being accepted is slim. But, with her mother's help, she manages to fix up a placement for herself. She has a number of her own pets -something that impresses the manager – and she isn't put off by the demanding and sometimes upsetting sides of animal care work – cold, wet, windy weather, a tiring round of exercising the dogs and cleaning out their kennels, seeing her favourite dog become sick and die. The book features a specialised area of work – one where temperament and vocation count for a lot – and some of the unpleasant features are described deliberately and realistically to discourage students who might think that working with dogs entails only the handling of nice, clean, cuddly puppies.

More topics are touched on in the narrative, and teachers are given 'prompts' at the top corner of each right-hand page to remind them of points they could develop as they read through the book.

PAGE BY PAGE NOTES FOR THE TEACHER

AN ANIMAL CHARITY: PAGE 1

- The teacher might introduce the book by asking which students have pets at home, their experiences and feelings towards them; then introduce the subject of unwanted or badly treated pets.
- Ask which students think they might be interested in working with animals.
- Talk about the sort of place Jessica has gone to work at – it's more than a dogs' home.
- Ask the students if they've ever been to an animal rescue centre or heard of the RSPCA, what the letters stand for, and what the organisation does.

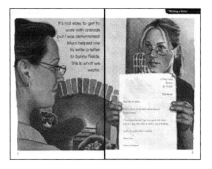

AN ANIMAL CHARITY: PAGES 2-3

- See the 'Arranging Your Own Placement' Interactive Activity - page 79.
- Talk about the letter Jessica has written and why it is necessary to take a lot of trouble to get things right.
- Spot the two cats and the hamster in the picture.

AN ANIMAL CHARITY: PAGES 4-5

- Interviews - what they're for and how they are conducted. (See the 'What Happens at an Interview' Interactive Activity - page 99).
- "It's not easy to get work with animals" (*An Animal Charity*, page 2). Ask the students how they think Jessica has managed to be given a placement. What has she said or done to make Mr Andrews think she will do well?
- Talk about tetanus injections, what they're for and if any of the students have had them and in what circumstances.
- Discuss attitudes to injections generally.

AN ANIMAL CHARITY: PAGES 6-7

- Study the illustration. Can the students pick out four types of animal looked after at Sunny Fields?
- Can they see where Jessica and Mr Andrews are heading for (the way the signpost is pointing)?
- Ask the students to think about how the animals came to be in the centre.

Resources for: 'An Animal Charity'

AN ANIMAL CHARITY: PAGES 8-9

- Study the three cameo illustrations. Get the students to think about why these animals have been treated like this. Many of the animals will be unwanted by their owners – possibly given as Christmas presents in the first place – and are now 'strays' that wander the streets.

AN ANIMAL CHARITY: PAGES 10-11

- Point out that Jessica will be working with the dogs that are ready for new homes – not the sick or injured ones that would require more expert handling.
- "Mr Andrews said I'd learn a lot by watching Ben". (*An Animal Charity* page 10.) Remind students that the point of work experience is to learn what is involved and to help them decide if they are suited to the job they're sampling.

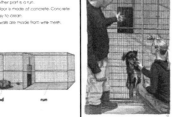

AN ANIMAL CHARITY: PAGES 12-13

- Discuss the design of the kennel, its size, the materials used and how it meets the needs of the dogs.
- See if the students notice the drop-down dividing door and the drain cover running left-to-right by Ben's left boot (the cleaning of the kennels appears later in the narrative).

AN ANIMAL CHARITY: PAGES 14-15

- Ask the students why they think the dogs were given their own names.
- Ask if any of the students have dogs and what breeds they are.
- Think up other names that are alliterative, like Bruno Boxer or Charlie Collie.

AN ANIMAL CHARITY: PAGES 16-17

- Few placements require the student to work beyond 4pm and we have allowed ourselves some licence here to highlight what *normal* working hours are and the tiredness that many students feel even when their hours are shorter.
- Test the students' attitude to working outdoors or in open-air conditions. (The issue of suitable clothing is raised on the next page).

Resources for: 'An Animal Charity'

AN ANIMAL CHARITY: PAGES 18-19

- See the 'Working with Animals' Interactive Activity (page 81) for a test of squeamishness and what it means – a good topic for discussion.
- See also 'Working Outdoors' Interactive Activity (page 80).

AN ANIMAL CHARITY: PAGES 20-23

- These pages deal with animal sickness, Bruno Boxer's sickness and death, and Jessica's feelings. It may offer teachers the opportunity to talk about these issues more widely.
- Discuss what vets do, and invite students to talk about their experiences with vets or their animals being injured or getting sick.

AN ANIMAL CHARITY: PAGE 24

- Students can discuss how well Jessica did (see the 'How Well Did Jesica Do?' Resource Sheet - page 89).
- Talk about opportunities for voluntary and unpaid work.
- Talk about animal care courses that may be available at the right level at college.
- See the 'Working with Animals' Interactive Activity (page 81) and a suitability test set for students.

Resources for: 'An Animal Charity'

INTERACTIVE ACTIVITIES

There are four interactive activities that develop key themes in the narrative. Like all the Interactive Activities in this course they are designed for use both on whiteboards and individual PCs.

1. ARRANGING YOUR OWN PLACEMENT

Jessica arranges her own placement (with her mother's help). Although most schools will have their list of suitable firms, there are occasions when particular students know what they want and arrange their own placements themselves. In this respect, Jessica is a useful role model for students to follow, and in this activity they are asked to look at such things as: the information they need to write a letter (manager's name, address and postcode), where to find it, how to write a good letter and address the envelope properly, compare this with a bad letter, what kind of stamp to put on and where to get it.

See page 79 for full details of this Interactive Activity.

2. WORKING OUTDOORS

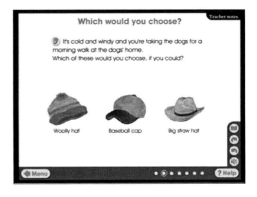

In the story Jessica is told to "wear old clothes". Students consider appropriate and inappropriate clothing for different kinds of outdoor work and different weather conditions.

See page 80 for full details of this Interactive Activity.

3. WORKING WITH ANIMALS

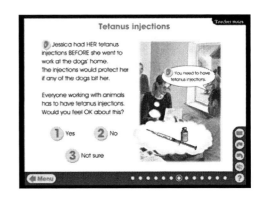

Jessica enjoys her work and has realistic expectations. In this activity, students' suitability for the job are tested rigorously – they are asked eight questions, such as: Do you have experience of looking after your own pets? Could you put up with cold, wet weather? Could you cope with having to have tetanus injections?

In the conclusion, they are shown their answers, and told that they would need to have answered 'yes' to most of the questions if they were going to succeed in a job with animals.

See page 81 for full details of this Interactive Activity.

78

1. 'ARRANGING YOUR OWN PLACEMENT' INTERACTIVE ACTIVITY TEACHER NOTES

RELATES TO: 'AN ANIMAL CHARITY' PAGES 2-5
LEVEL: 1-3

NB Some schools already encourage *able* students to make choices about their placements and to go through the process of telephoning, writing letters, fixing up an interview by themselves, though with help.

OBJECTIVES

Students will learn to:
- Apply letter writing skills to a real-life situation.
- Think about the *content* of a good letter.
- Use their research skills to find out the details they need – for instance, the manager's name, the address and postcode of the work place – using the telephone or internet.
- Address the envelope correctly and where they can buy stamps.
- Think about suitable placements and make choices for themselves.
- Use their own initiative.

FOLLOW-UP ACTIVITIES

- Letter writing practice and addressing envelopes.
- Improving research skills using telephone directories, the internet.
- Invite *Connexions* staff to talk about different work placements and how they can be arranged. (Go to www.connexions-direct.com for details.)
- Practice in using the telephone in real and role play situations.

2. 'WORKING OUTDOORS' INTERACTIVE ACTIVITY TEACHER NOTES

RELATES TO: 'AN ANIMAL CHARITY' PAGES 4, 16, 19

LEVEL: 1-2

(The four 'sorting' exercises are graded. It is advisable that the student tackles them in order.)

OBJECTIVES

Students will learn about:

- Appropriate clothing for a range of outdoor work.
- Clothing appropriate to different types of weather.
- Different types of outdoor work.
- What to expect if they choose outdoor work.

FOLLOW-UP ACTIVITIES

- Students – with help, if needed – gather together appropriate clothing for a given situation.
- Students learn to watch the weather forecast on the television and choose appropriate clothing for the next day.
- Students find out more about measuring temperature, using a thermometer etc.
- If their work experience is in the summer, they find out about how best to protect their skin against exposure to the sun.
- Students find out what special clothing will be supplied on their work placement, if any, and which clothing they will need to provide themselves.

NOTE: students may not have the right items of clothing suggested here and may need help with providing the essentials.

3. 'WORKING WITH ANIMALS' INTERACTIVE ACTIVITY TEACHER NOTES

> **RELATES TO: 'AN ANIMAL CHARITY' PAGES 1-24**
>
> **LEVEL: 1-2**
>
> ## OBJECTIVES
>
> Students will gain a better understanding of:
> - What is involved in working at an animal rescue centre.
> - Those aspects of the work they may not have thought of: long hours; tiredness; wintry weather; tetanus injections; the smelly, dirty work; animal cruelty; sickness and death of animals.
> - Their own suitability.
> - The experience of animals that family pets provide.
>
> ## FOLLOW-UP ACTIVITIES
>
> - Run through the book a second time looking at what was involved in Jessica's work.
> - Get students who have pets to explain how they look after them and what is involved.
> - Look at other potential work places where animals need looking after eg a veterinary practice, a zoo, a farm, stables, and what might be involved in each.
> - Examine the 'plus' sides of working with animals.
> - Devise role play situations.

RESOURCE SHEETS FOR THE STUDENT

You may copy these sheets freely for use in your school.

There are seven resource sheets which relate specifically to *An Animal Charity*:

1. HOW WELL DID YOU READ?

Ten simple true or false questions related to the text.

2. KEYWORD FLASHCARDS

Sixteen work-related words taken from the text. These need to be printed onto card and cut up.

3. WORDSEARCH

Ten key words chosen from the sixteen flashcards.

4. SPOT THE DIFFERENCE

An illustration from the book with six details changed.

5. THE BOOK AND ACTIVITIES: WHAT I THOUGHT OF THEM

Students write a sentence or two giving their views on the book and activities they've just tackled and think about anything they might have learned.

6. HOW WELL DID JESSICA DO?

Students look at Jessica from Mr Andrew's point of view, and fill in a form about her attitude and performance.

7. STUDENT'S RECORD SHEET

A record sheet for the teacher to record the various activities undertaken by the student in this part of the course, and the level achieved.

There are also these additional sheets for the Work Experience course as a whole:

A. DETAILS OF MY PLACEMENT

A form or checklist for the student to fill in *before* his/her placement begins. It brings together all the main information the student will need.

B. MY WORK EXPERIENCE: HOW I GOT ON

An evaluation form students will complete *after* their placement. It will give them an opportunity to say how they got on, what they learned, and what they liked or didn't like.

Work Experience: An Animal Charity

How well did you read?

Five of these are TRUE, and five are FALSE.

1. Jessica wanted to work with animals.	TRUE / FALSE
2. Her dad helped her to write a letter.	TRUE / FALSE
3. She had a boxer dog called Shep.	TRUE / FALSE
4. She had to have a tetanus injection.	TRUE / FALSE
5. Mr Andrews told her to bring a packed lunch.	TRUE / FALSE
6. Her supervisor was called Tony.	TRUE / FALSE
7. Her favourite dog was called Bruno.	TRUE / FALSE
8. Jessica was given green overalls to wear.	TRUE / FALSE
9. The wind blew off her woolly hat.	TRUE / FALSE
10. Mr Andrews gave her a full-time job.	TRUE / FALSE

© SEN Press 2007. All rights reserved.

Key words flashcards

animal	charity
dog	cat
walk	kennel
clean	wrong

© SEN Press 2007. All rights reserved.

Key words flashcards

gloves	work
supervisor	home
weather	phone
injection	college

Wordsearch

Work Experience: An Animal Charity

Search for the hidden words from the lists in this grid.

v	d	h	q	w	t	b	p	c	m	r	y
d	o	g	e	r	c	k	o	a	o	h	u
c	l	a	b	o	m	x	s	t	r	y	e
l	g	d	d	n	f	g	l	o	v	e	s
h	e	g	s	g	e	m	f	k	i	i	o
f	d	j	s	i	z	h	s	e	n	c	p
c	h	a	r	i	t	y	k	n	g	l	w
e	k	s	v	h	q	e	l	n	m	o	a
c	j	a	q	u	d	a	i	e	s	t	l
c	l	e	a	n	v	g	o	l	e	h	k
f	a	j	h	w	o	r	k	o	q	e	v
a	n	i	m	a	l	r	j	q	e	t	b

animal   kennel
charity   clean
dog   wrong
cat   gloves
walk   work

© SEN Press 2007. All rights reserved.

Spot the difference

Can you spot the six differences in the pictures? Ring them on the picture on the right.

The book and activities feedback sheet

1. Say what you thought of the book.
(Could you read it and understand it? Did you find it interesting? A bit? Was it boring? Did you like any of the illustrations? Which one(s)?)

....

....

....

2. Say what you thought of the interactive activities.
(Did you find them easy to use? Did you enjoy any of them? Which one(s)?)

....

....

....

3. Say if you learned anything from either.

....

....

....

....

© SEN Press 2007. All rights reserved.

Work Experience: An Animal Charity

How well did Jessica do?

Imagine you are Mr Andrews filling in a form about Jessica. How do you think he would answer these questions?

1. Did she do what she was asked? Yes/No
2. Was she good with the animals? Yes/No
3. Was she sensible? Yes/No
4. Did she work hard? Yes/No
5. Did she have the right attitude? Yes/No
6. Did you have to tick her off for any reason? Yes/No

If "Yes", say what it was for:

....

....

....

Other comments:

....

....

....

....

© SEN Press 2007. All rights reserved.

Student record sheet

An Animal Charity

……………………………………………………………………….has,

- Read the text - with help/without help
- Made a contribution to the discussion - yes/no
- Completed the *How well did you read*? exercise - with help/without help
  Score:…………………………
- Tackled the 16 flashcards and achieved this score:…………………
- Completed these interactive activities
  - Arranging your own placement
  - Working outdoors
  - Working with animals

- Completed these research or follow-up activities:

  - ……………………………………………………………………
  - ……………………………………………………………………

- Completed these other resource sheets:
  - Wordsearch
  - Spot the difference
  - How well did Jessica do?
  - Book and activities feedback sheet

- Any other achievements or lessons learned:………………………….

……………………………………………………………………………

……………………………………………………………………………

……………………………………………………………………………

……………………………………………………………………………

© SEN Press 2007. All rights reserved.

Resources for: 'An Animal Charity'

The following two generic resource sheets are also relevant to this book.

Full size worksheets for copying can be found on pages 111-112 of this book.

Work Experience

Details of my placement

My placement is at:..

Address:..
....

Tel no:...

My supervisor's name:..

My start time:...............am

My finish time:...............pm

How I will get to work:..
....

Time I will leave home:...............am

Things I will take with me..
....

Lunchtime will be at:..

My short breaks will be at ....and..................... and be for
............minutes.

For lunch I will...

At work, I will be doing these things:................................
....

Rules I must remember:..
....
....
....

© SEN Press 2007. All rights reserved.

Work Experience

My Work Experience: how I got on

I worked at:...

Dates:..

Type of work place (factory? shop? etc):.........................
....

A description of what went on there:................................
....

What I did:..
....

What I liked about it:..
....

What I didn't like about it:...
....

What I learned:...
....
....
....

Teacher's remarks:..
....
....
....

© SEN Press 2007. All rights reserved.

RESOURCES FOR 'AN INTERVIEW'

'AN INTERVIEW'

WORK EXPERIENCE SERIES

LEVEL: 1-2

READING AGE: 7.0 – 8.0 YEARS

24 PAGES

749 WORDS

KEY THEMES

Finding the way.
Arriving at Reception.
Punctuality.
First impressions.
Body language.
Listening to and answering questions.
An opportunity to ask questions.

THE NARRATIVE

The book is set out as a play with two parts – Mr Kemp and Paul.

In one of the Interactive Activities on the CD (*What Happens at an Interview*) it will be possible to recreate and practise an interview with different names. It is suggested that the teacher should take the part of Mr Kemp, and the student take the part of Paul. This way the amount of reading for the student is more than halved.

The title looks at the key elements of an interview, and students are able to study Paul – through his words and the illustrations – and the parts of the interview he gets either right or wrong. He starts, like most students, shy and awkward but his good points are drawn out by Mr Kemp who is prepared to give him a chance. Paul's mobile phone ringing in the middle of the interview is a reminder of what is and isn't allowed at work.

More issues are touched on in the narrative, and teachers are given 'prompts' at the top corner of each right-hand page to remind them of points they could develop as they read through the book.

Resources for: 'An Interview'

PAGE BY PAGE NOTES FOR THE TEACHER

AN INTERVIEW: PAGE 1

- See if the students can guess what the sign on the warehouse says [(Ga)rden has its first two letters missing].
- Pages 20 to 21 tell us what goes on there, but it would be helpful to establish what happens in warehouses generally, and how they differ from factories.

AN INTERVIEW: PAGES 2-3

- This scene offers students the opportunity to find out how they will get to their interview, and if someone will be going with them.

AN INTERVIEW: PAGES 4-5

- This illustration offers an opportunity to talk about how people find their way to new places without getting lost – by noticing and recording landmarks.
- Ask the students to point out the landmarks.
- Listen to their concerns about getting lost, missing their stop etc.

AN INTERVIEW: PAGES 6-7

- Students will benefit from being taken over this standard procedure of entering a strange building for an interview (or any other purpose), and reporting to Reception.
- See the 'Golden Rules' ('Be Punctual') Interactive Activity - page 6 - which underlines the need to arrive a few minutes early.

93

Resources for: 'An Interview'

AN INTERVIEW: PAGES 8-9

- Students should be prepared for an initial handshake and to look the interviewer in the eye. They may not be offered a drink if they are on their own, but probably will if a teaching assistant is accompanying them.

AN INTERVIEW: PAGES 10-11

- Clarify the term "body language". Students will be given an opportunity to be taken through an interview in the Interactive Activity 'What Happens at an Interview' - page 99.

AN INTERVIEW: PAGES 12-13

- Find out which students have mobile phones.
- Consider times when mobile phones should be switched off.

AN INTERVIEW: PAGES 14-15

- Mr Kemp doesn't get very good answers from Paul when his questions are about school, but gets much fuller, more confident answers when he asks about hobbies and home life.

AN INTERVIEW: PAGES 16-17

- Mr Kemp is probably impressed to hear that Paul takes responsibility for his younger brother.

Resources for: 'An Interview'

AN INTERVIEW: PAGES 18-19

- Mr Kemp mentions training at work that can offer young people with poor academic performance a chance to learn while they work.

AN INTERVIEW: PAGES 20-21

- Discuss what sort of firm *Garden World* is and what is likely to go on in the warehouse.

- Notice the Health & Safety poster on the wall. Ask the students what sort of health and safety issues might apply in the warehouse.

- Do the students understand what fork-lift trucks are and what they do?

AN INTERVIEW: PAGES 22-23

- Paul learns what he will be doing by showing an interest and asking questions.

AN INTERVIEW: PAGE 24

- Evaluate Paul's performance (see 'How Well did Paul do at Interview?' Resource Sheet for students to complete - page 107.)
- Discuss Paul and his qualities and if he was suitable for the job.
- Ask what students think of the job and if they'd like to work there.
- Find out which bits did and did not appeal.
- Think about a) what Mr Kemp has learned about Paul and b) what Paul has learned about Mr Kemp and the warehouse.

Resources for: 'An Interview'

INTERACTIVE ACTIVITIES

There are three interactive activities that develop key themes in the narrative. They are designed for use both on whiteboards and individual PCs.

1. GETTING THERE ON TIME

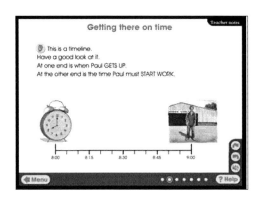

This activity focuses on Paul's arrival for interview on time, suggesting time planning.

Students are made to think about leaving enough time in the morning to arrive at work on time. They are given an alarm clock which is due to go off at 8 o'clock.

They are also given a morning routine of: shower (15 minutes), get dressed (5 minutes), have breakfast (10 minutes) and so on, and the question is: will they have left enough time to get to work by 9.00am?

They have to drag each block of time onto a timeline in order to find out, and change the setting of the alarm if they find they haven't left themselves enough time.

See page 97 for full details of this Interactive Activity.

2. GIVING A GOOD IMPRESSION

This activity relates to Paul's first meeting with Mr Kemp. Students are asked to consider a number of different factors that would affect Mr Kemp's first impression.

See page 98 for full details of this Interactive Activity.

3. WHAT HAPPENS AT AN INTERVIEW

This activity requires the teacher to take the part of the interviewer, and the student(s) to practise their answers to a similar set of questions as the book. The CD-ROM provides audio-prompts for the student, suggesting what they might say. It could work well as a group activity following the whiteboard presentation.

See page 99 for full details of this Interactive Activity.

1. 'GETTING THERE ON TIME' INTERACTIVE ACTIVITY TEACHER NOTES

RELATES TO: 'AN INTERVIEW' PAGES 6-7

LEVEL: 2

OBJECTIVES

(Involves the calculation of time. Many students will need help.)

Students will learn:

- An everyday, practical use for a timeline.
- A way of working backwards from a start time.
- The need for a (morning) routine that will get them to get to a destination on time.
- How long their morning routine takes.
- That they will have to do this by themselves at some stage.

FOLLOW-UP ACTIVITIES

- Students talk about their own morning routines, calculate times and plot them on a timeline.
- Students do similar calculations for an evening deadline after getting home from school/college (eg going to the cinema).

OTHER POINTS

- As in 'Golden Rules' (*A Supermarket* Interactive Activity, see page 6), it should be pointed out that punctuality for work (and a number of other situations) involves arriving 5-10 minutes early, leaving time for washing, going to the toilet etc and being ready for work at the stated time
- It will need to be explained to students that people's morning routines and means of getting to work can be very different. I daresay most students will skip the shower, breakfast, teeth-cleaning and give themselves another half an hour in bed!

Resources for: 'An Interview'

2. 'GIVING A GOOD IMPRESSION' INTERACTIVE ACTIVITY TEACHER NOTES

RELATES TO: 'AN INTERVIEW' PAGES 1-24

LEVEL: 1-2

OBJECTIVES

Students consider:

- What 'giving a good impression' means.
- How to give a good first impression themselves.
- How to present themselves for interview.
- Good and bad body language.
- Good and bad answers.
- The importance of punctuality.

FOLLOW-UP ACTIVITIES

- Go through the text and illustrations a second time, evaluating Paul's performance and the impression he is giving to Mr Kemp.
- Discuss appropriate clothing for interview.
- Practise sitting correctly.
- Practise looking at each other in the eye while talking.
- Practise shaking hands and saying hello with a smile.

3. 'WHAT HAPPENS AT AN INTERVIEW' INTERACTIVE ACTIVITY TEACHER NOTES

RELATES TO: 'AN INTERVIEW' PAGES 1-24
LEVEL: 1-2

OBJECTIVES

Students learn
- How to face the person interviewing them confidently, to shake hands, to smile and say hello.
- The basic form that an interview takes (first greeting, sitting down for questions, being shown round etc).
- To listen attentively to the questions.
- To think about what they'll say about themselves and practise saying it.
- To recognise the same basic question asked in different ways.
- To develop short answers into longer, more confident answers.

FOLLOW-UP ACTIVITY

Note: this is a role play activity and can be used as a first run-through after reading the book.

The teacher will probably have taken the part of Mr Kemp, and the part of Paul by one or more students. As a follow-up, it would be good to put the students through a similar experience.

Resources for: 'An Interview'

RESOURCE SHEETS FOR THE STUDENT

You may copy these sheets freely for use in your school.

There are nine resource sheets which relate specifically to *An Interview*:

1. HOW WELL DID YOU READ?

Ten simple true or false questions related to the text.

2. KEYWORD FLASHCARDS

Sixteen work-related words taken from the text. These need to be printed onto card and cut up.

3. WORDSEARCH

Ten key words chosen from the sixteen flashcards.

4. SPOT THE DIFFERENCE

An illustration from the book with six details changed.

5. THE BOOK AND ACTIVITIES: WHAT I THOUGHT OF THEM

Students write a sentence or two giving their views on the book and activities they've just tackled and think about anything they might have learned.

6. HOW WELL DID PAUL DO?

Students look at Paul from Mr Kemp's point of view, and fill in a form about his attitude and performance.

7. MY INTERVIEW

A form or checklist for the students to fill in *before* an interview takes place. It brings together all the main information they will need to find out.

8. MY INTERVIEW: HOW I GOT ON

An evaluation form students will complete *after* an interview. It will give them an opportunity to say how they think they got on, what they learned, and how they could do better next time.

9. STUDENT'S RECORD SHEET

A record sheet for the teacher to record the various activities undertaken by the student in this part of the course, and the level achieved.

There are also these additional sheets for the Work Experience course as a whole:

A. DETAILS OF MY PLACEMENT

A form or checklist for the student to fill in *before* his/her placement begins. It brings together all the main information the student will need.

B. MY WORK EXPERIENCE: HOW I GOT ON

An evaluation form students will complete *after* their placement. It will give them an opportunity to say how they got on, what they learned, and what they liked or didn't like.

Work Experience: An Interview

How well did you read?

Five of these are TRUE, and five are FALSE.

1. Paul was going to an interview.   TRUE / FALSE

2. He went by himself.   TRUE / FALSE

3. The warehouse was called Garden World.   TRUE / FALSE

4. He got there by bus.   TRUE / FALSE

5. He was five minutes late.   TRUE / FALSE

6. He rang the bell at Reception.   TRUE / FALSE

7. Mr Kemp wore a suit and tie.   TRUE / FALSE

8. Paul said he liked sport the best.   TRUE / FALSE

9. His mobile phone rang during the interview.   TRUE / FALSE

10. Mr Kemp said Paul could have a go on the fork-lift truck.   TRUE / FALSE

© SEN Press 2007. All rights reserved.

Work Experience: An Interview

Key words flashcards

interview	warehouse
bus	station
drawing	teacher
barcode	label

© SEN Press 2007. All rights reserved.

Key words flashcards

fork-lift	rule
private	staff only
manager	behave
mobile phone	training

© SEN Press 2007. All rights reserved.

Wordsearch

Work Experience: An Interview

Search for the hidden words from the lists in this grid.

z	d	b	u	w	t	b	u	s	p	r	w
g	k	x	h	r	u	l	e	a	k	q	a
i	n	t	e	r	v	i	e	w	r	y	r
l	g	d	d	n	f	g	l	a	b	z	e
g	e	p	j	o	m	n	f	n	a	i	h
t	e	a	c	h	e	r	f	t	r	c	o
k	t	g	a	n	t	d	k	o	c	l	u
f	o	r	k	l	i	f	t	r	o	a	s
h	c	a	c	u	b	a	i	b	d	b	e
d	r	a	w	i	n	g	o	l	e	l	r
d	h	k	p	q	n	m	k	o	q	e	l
s	t	a	t	i	o	n	j	q	e	i	a

interview teacher
warehouse barcode
bus label
station fork-lift
drawing rule

© SEN Press 2007. All rights reserved.

Spot the difference

Can you spot the six differences in the pictures? Ring them on the picture on the right.

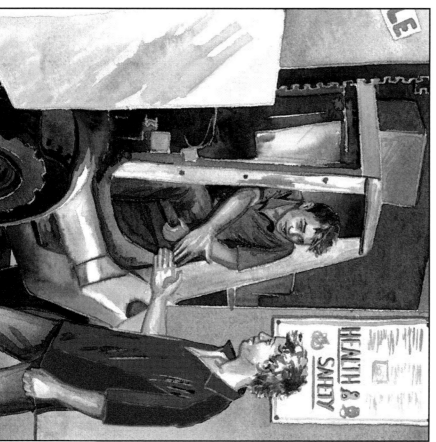

Work Experience: An Interview

Work Experience: An Interview

The book and activities feedback sheet

1. Say what you thought of the book.
(Could you read it and understand it? Did you find it interesting? A bit? Was it boring? Did you like any of the illustrations? Which one(s)?)

....

....

....

2. Say what you thought of the interactive activities.
(Did you find them easy to use? Did you enjoy any of them? Which one(s)?)

....

....

....

3. Say if you learned anything from either.

....

....

....

....

© SEN Press 2007. All rights reserved.

How well did Paul do?

Imagine you are Mr Kemp filling in a form about Paul. How do you think he would answer these questions?

1.	Was he punctual for his interview?	Yes/No
2.	Was he polite?	Yes/No
3.	Did he give a good first impression?	Yes/No
4.	Did he show interest and ask questions?	Yes/No
5.	Did he have the right attitude?	Yes/No
6.	Do you think he will do well on work experience?	Yes/No

If "Yes", please say why:

....

....

....

Other comments:

....

....

....

....

© SEN Press 2007. All rights reserved.

Work Experience

My interview

My interview is at:……………………………………………………………………

Address:………………………………………………………………………………

………………………………………………………………………………………

Time of interview:……………………

Time I will try to get there:………………

Time I will set off:……………………

Name of person I'm meeting:………………………………………………………

How I will get there:………………………………………………………………

………………………………………………………………………………………

What I will wear:……………………………………………………………………

What I will take with me:……………………………………………………………

………………………………………………………………………………………

How I will give a good impression:…………………………………………………

………………………………………………………………………………………

………………………………………………………………………………………

Other things I need to remember:……………………………………………………

………………………………………………………………………………………

………………………………………………………………………………………

………………………………………………………………………………………

© SEN Press 2007. All rights reserved.

Work Experience

My interview: how I got on

I went to interview at:……………………………………………………

Date:………………………………………………………………………

I was interviewed by:……………………………………………………

Type of work place (factory? shop? etc):………………………………

A description of what went on there:……………………………………
………………………………………………………………………………

What I was asked about:…………………………………………………
………………………………………………………………………………

How well I think I did:……………………………………………………
………………………………………………………………………………

What I learned:……………………………………………………………
………………………………………………………………………………

How I could do better next time:…………………………………………
………………………………………………………………………………
………………………………………………………………………………

Teacher's remarks:…………………………………………………………
………………………………………………………………………………
………………………………………………………………………………
………………………………………………………………………………

© SEN Press 2007. All rights reserved.

Work Experience: An Interview

Student record sheet

An Interview

....has,

- Read the text - with help/without help
- Made a contribution to the discussion - yes/no
- Completed the *How well did you read*? exercise - with help/without help
  Score:...............................
- Tackled the 16 flashcards and achieved this score:....................
- Completed these interactive activities
  - Giving a good impression
  - What happens at an interview
  - Getting there on time

- Completed these research or follow-up activities:

  - ....
  - ....

- Completed these other resource sheets:
  - Wordsearch
  - Spot the difference
  - How well did Paul do?
  - Book and activities feedback sheet

- Any other achievements or lessons learned:....................................

....

....

....

© SEN Press 2007. All rights reserved.

Details of my placement

My placement is at...

Address:..

....

Tel no:.....................................

My supervisor's name:...

My start time:...............am

My finish time:...............pm

How I will get to work:...

....

Time I will leave home:...............am

Things I will take with me..

....

Lunchtime will be at:.....................................

My short breaks will be at ....and..................... and be for ....minutes.

For lunch I will...

At work, I will be doing these things:..

....

Rules I must remember:..

....

....

....

© SEN Press 2007. All rights reserved.

My Work Experience: how I got on

I worked at..

Dates:..

Type of work place (factory? shop? etc):..................................
....

A description of what went on there:...
....

What I did:..
....

What I liked about it:..
....

What I didn't like about it:..
....

What I learned:..
....
....
....

Teacher's remarks:..
....
....
....

© SEN Press 2007. All rights reserved.